# BETWEEN
# NOON
# AND
# THREE

# BETWEEN NOON AND THREE

## A Parable of Romance, Law, and the Outrage of Grace

### ROBERT FARRAR CAPON

*1817*

Harper & Row, Publishers, San Francisco

Cambridge, Hagerstown, New York, Philadelphia
London, Mexico City, São Paulo, Sydney

Acknowledgment is made for the following: Quotations from FOUR QUAR-
TETS by T. S. Eliot, reprinted by permission of Harcourt Brace Jovanovich,
Inc. Quotations from THE ELDER STATESMAN by T. S. Eliot, © 1959, by
permission of Farrar, Straus, & Giroux, Inc. Quotations from W. H. AUDEN:
COLLECTED POEMS, by W. H. Auden, edited by Edward Mendelson, © by
Edward Mendelson, William Meredith, and Monroe K. Spears, executors of
the estate of W. H. Auden, by permission of Random House, Inc.

FIRST EDITION

*Designer: Jim Mennick*

---

**Library of Congress Cataloging in Publication Data**

Capon, Robert Farrar.
   BETWEEN NOON AND THREE.

   1. Grace (Theology). 2. Law and gospel. 3. Ethics. 4. Sexual ethics.
I. Title.
BT761.2.C33   1982     234     81–47832
ISBN 0–06–061308–4        AACR2

---

82  83  84  85  86  10  9  8  7  6  5  4  3  2  1

*To the praise of the glory*
*of his grace*
*(Eph. 1:6)*

# Contents

# PART I

# *Parable*

# 1

By and by I want to tell you a story. It will be about a man and a woman who actually succeed in getting away with something. I think I shall make him a university professor and her a suburban housewife finishing some long-interrupted work on a master's in English. Paul, perhaps, will do for his name; forty, tall, dark, handsome. And for hers? Linda? No, Linda is a waitress with a sad, uncomprehended history of failed romances. Laura? Yes, Laura; thirty-five, intelligent, chestnut-haired and beautiful. I insist on proper romantic types. I want nothing unconventional here except the success of the affair.

That is a promise. I shall allow not a single development that might in any way take the edge off their triumph. No divorces, no automobile accidents, no erotic failures, no natural disasters. I shall make them immune from headache, pique, curdled moods and the common cold. I shall even make them religious, but leave them happily unburdened by scruples. You will be spared those tiresome scenes in which lovers fill the pauses of their passion with lugubrious wonderings about whether they are failing their spouses, their children, or God. Better yet, you will not even have to endure the tension of wondering whether they will fail each other. They will not. I shall make the affair his last and her first: chastened experience will meet aroused innocence and, like giant smiling at giant, bring off the improbable with style. Best of all, they will not be discovered, ever.

They, of course, will not know that. But you and I do, and that is all that counts. For this story is about grace. I will have no tensions here except the tension of grace itself, no other scandal than the divine foolishness by which the human race is assured, in full and in advance, that there is nothing it isn't going to get away with— except disbelief in that assurance.

Do you find that odd? I hope so. But I also hope you find it odd for the right reason. A story such as I propose is bound to be unsatisfactory if either you or I look to it for a novelistic enrichment of our fantasy life. It will simply be—well, let us be honest—too uneventful. The true romantic novel requires conflict, comedy, danger and, ultimately, tragedy. In the end, the protagonists must be made to bear the disdain of a universe whose final reaction to the *O Altitudo* of romantic love is the snubbing stare it reserves for unimportantly disreputable performances, like spilling soup at a banquet.

For in our fantasies, immorality can never be allowed simply to succeed; cosmic disapproval must be given the last word. The assignation is accomplished, but the lover's water pump breaks down on the way home, necessitating a call to his wife to pick him up thirty miles off course. The beloved gives herself entirely, but her husband's firm moves him to Dallas and, out of the very givingness for which she is loved, she packs up dolls and dishes and goes sadly into the sunset. Or she loses a child in a fire that starts while she is in the motel with her lover. Or her lover loses his nerve. Or they marry at terrible cost and both lose their interest. Whatever happens, the books are always balanced, the notes due called in, the mortgages foreclosed.

No, much as you and I prefer that sort of thing, I shall not give it to you. First, because it is a strange preference no matter how universal it is. You would think, given the routinely low level of our performances at the higher reaches of our being, that we would, in our fantasies at least, welcome a respite from these inexorable audits, that we would imagine for ourselves romances in which the celestial bookkeeping department was given a long and well-deserved vacation. But no, we put it on overtime instead; however much we hate the law, we are more afraid of grace.

Oh, I know. You will say that the broken water pump or the child burned in the fire are simply elements of conflict or suspense introduced for the sake of proper dramatic development. I let that pass. Perhaps they are. My point here is that, novelistic development aside, they are in one respect totally unnecessary and in another necessary for a reason we have yet to face.

They are unnecessary because, if we are the least bit interested in holding up our imaginings as a mirror to real life, mishap and mischance are simply not going to appear in our glass with anything like the frequency you imply. We do in fact get away with almost everything. The one time my water pump broke, I was on business and still arrived at my meeting a minute early. I have not yet been in my first fire, or had anyone close to me in his. And neither, perhaps, have you—with only minor allowances for difference of circumstance. *Eppur si muove.* While it works at all, the contraption of the real world works very well indeed, and with practically no regard for moral necessities. The sun shines on the just and the unjust. A successful exercise in shacking up need not necessarily be any more improbable than a successful vichyssoise. A rarer treat, perhaps; but not the impossibility we so morbidly expect.

Therefore, the inevitability with which, in our fictions, the heroine makes infallible soup but tragic love derives from some other exigency than the pressure of events. It stems not from the universe but from our view of it. We are uneasy with the grace of a simply successful love affair not because it is unrealistically dull, but because it is all too obviously dangerous. It threatens to blow apart the imagined framework by which we hold ourselves, however inconveniently, in one piece. As long as the law is upon us we feel safe. Its bitching, score-evening presence assures us that something out there has our number. Whether it approves or disapproves of us is almost a matter of indifference; the main thing is that, having our number, it absolves us from the burden of learning our name. The law of retribution reigns supreme in our fantasies precisely to keep us off the main question of our lives: *What would you do with freedom if you had it?*

Our romantic imaginings are designed specifically to frustrate our principal exploration. With a perversity we would never permit in a discussion of cookery, we resolutely disallow the success of the romantic omelette and concentrate upon—no, it must be stronger: we revel in, we preoccupy ourselves with—the imagined necessities by which the stove must go cold, the pan crack, the eggs corrupt, the butter putrefy. For all its trappings of reality, however, the lion we thus see in the way of our self-discovery is philosophical, not real. As long as we give it credence, we give it power; but one straight look and it is gone.

And that is the second, and the important reason why I propose to give you the story of a triumphantly, even boringly successful adultery. Grace cannot prevail until law is dead; there is no way of seeing clearly the freedom to which we are being driven until morality has been bound, gagged and stuffed unceremoniously in the trunk. That is the fundamental oddity of our condition and, while there is no way of tempering its oddness, there are at least precedents to keep us from expecting it to go away.

The classic parables of grace always involve the flaunting of some immorality, some inequity, some gratuitously offensive detail. The father's free acceptance of the prodigal son is not fully portrayed until he orders the slaying of the fatted calf—and the elder brother rightly observes that all his years of goodness never got him even a goat. The gracious beneficence of the owner of the vineyard is not driven home until those who worked but one hour are paid, not only equally with the rest, but ahead of them as well. The good Samaritan is simply an insult: to Jesus' Jewish audience there were no good Samaritans; to make a hero of one was to stand truth on its head.

Let me refine that a little. I said grace cannot prevail until law is dead, until moralizing is out of the game. The precise phrase should be: until our fatal love affair with the law is over, until, finally and for good, our lifelong certainty that someone is keeping score has run out of steam and collapsed. As long as you leave, in your parable of grace, one single hope of a moral reckoning, one possible recourse to salvation by bookkeeping, our freedom-dreading hearts will clutch it to themselves. And even if you leave none at all, we will grub for ethics that are not there rather than face the liberty to which grace calls us. Give us the parable of the prodigal son, for example, and we will promptly lose its point by preaching ourselves sermons on worthy and unworthy confession or on the sin of the elder brother. Give us the workers in the vineyard, and we will concoct spurious lessons on the duty of contentment or the moral aspects of labor relations.

Restore to us, Preacher, the comfort of merit and demerit. Prove for us that there is at least something we can do, that we are still, at whatever dim recess of our nature, the masters of our relationships. Tell us, Prophet, that in spite of all our nights of losing, there will yet be one redeeming card of our very own to fill the inside straight we have so long and so earnestly tried to draw to. But do not preach us grace. It will not do to split the pot evenly at four in the morning and break out the Chivas Regal. We insist on being reckoned with. Give us something, anything; but spare us the indignity of this indiscriminate acceptance.

Lord, let your servants depart in the peace of their proper responsibility. If it is not too much to ask, send us to bed with some few shreds of self-respect to congratulate ourselves upon. But if that is too hard, leave us at least the consolation of our self-loathing. Only do not force us free. What have we ever done but try as best we could? How have we so hurt you, even by failing, that you should now turn on us and say that none of it makes any difference, not even our sacred guilt? We have played this game of yours and it has cost us.

*Where do you get off suggesting a drink at a time like this?*

[ 8 ]

## 2

I know. I have overstated things slightly. But only
slightly. In any case, enough of that for the time being.

*           *           *

It was just before noon on the first warm day of April.
Paul swung his '74 Nova into the left lane, waited out the
light, and turned into the restaurant parking lot. Laura
was standing in front of some junipers by the main door.
He pulled the car into a space at the side and walked
around to meet her.

"I hope you haven't been waiting long. Are you always this early?"

"Only when I want to be. The official line on me is
that I'm a scatterbrain. I'm supposed not to be able to find
places or tell time. Don't blow my cover."

"I wouldn't think of it. Especially not on the first
date."

He guided her into the restaurant with his hand on
the small of her back. Seats. Waitress. Conference on
drinks: two Cinzano Red, twist, no ice, please. Sorry Sir,
no Cinzano. All right, two Martini & Rossi, same. Have
to ask the bartender . . . sorry, no Martini & Rossi; how
about Duval? No, thank you. Two Dubonnet. Nobody
doesn't have Dubonnet.

She sat watching, elbows on the table, chin resting on

clasped hands, her eyes moving between him and the waitress.

"You're a flirt, you know," she said after the girl left.

He put on a chastened look. "Damn! Found out even before lunch."

"Oh, it's all right. It's just your style. You act as if you and the person you're talking to have the same inside joke in the back of your minds. It's . . . flattering."

"Usually, I'm told I don't really pay attention to people."

"That's probably true too. You have lots of styles. I was just telling you about a nice one."

When the waitress came with the drinks, he lifted his glass. "Well! To me for finally having asked you out; to you for saying yes—and to your master's program for having suggested it in the first place."

She clinked her glass against his. "I'll be glad when *that* part's over. I'm tired of fighting with Irving Schiff-mann. He's having an absolute fit, you know, over my insistence that Reilly, Alex and Julia in *The Cocktail Party* are actually angels. If I do any more Eliot, I want to stay clear of him."

"Irv has his blind spots, but he's a damned good judge of what is and isn't poetry. He's mostly right about Eliot's later stuff, *The Elder Statesman* for instance. Except for the one speech that makes the main point, it's pretty thin."

"The *Quartets* aren't."

"Agreed. Just don't write Irv off. In any case, though, what are you going to do after you get the degree?"

"I don't know. Auden, maybe; though I'm not sure where I want to go with him. I just don't want to have to apologize all the time for trying to do something with what's really there."

"You thinking of a doctorate?"

She sipped her Dubonnet and made a little ritual of centering the glass and the cocktail napkin between the flatware.

"Not yet. If I can, I want to go back to teaching full time. For now I'd just like to work to the point at which I had a master's plus thirty. If a good idea for a thesis turns up, so much the better."

He put down his glass, reached for the breadbasket, hesitated, then settled for arranging it at right angles to her knife.

"Funny," he said. "Breadbasket to Knife 4. Black's classic response to the Centered Glass opening. Did you ever read that piece in the *New Yorker* about the middle-aged man who was having lunch with his father? The actual conversation just pooped along, but they kept out-maneuvering each other with the objects on the table: ashtrays, salt shakers, glasses. Their real relationship came across in the analogy to chess. Clever."

"I didn't see it, but that's true. It's the moves that count."

She smiled, picked up her knife, and put it on her bread and butter plate pointing toward him.

"There. What does black do now?"

"Easy. I offer a course on Auden in September."

She repeated the word "September" in exactly his tone of voice.

"Wouldn't you be interested?" he asked, thrown off by her response.

"Of course."

"Then why did you hesitate?"

"I didn't hesitate; you did. This is April."

"Hmm," he said. "I seem to be in check. Well, let me ask you something. Where does your husband . . . fit in?"

"He loves me without liking me, I guess. That happens. We deal with each other mostly on the level of house and children. It's a kind of civil standoff."

"How long has it been like that?"

"From the beginning. Although when you're first married, you don't pay attention to it. I didn't admit it to myself for about three years, but eventually it became obvious it had been like that all along. The trouble is, he doesn't realize it even now. He simply doesn't know what's happening. He resents my interests, but he can't admit it because he has none of his own to fall back on. And there's no use my becoming a zero just to keep him company."

She took a drink, then looked up and continued.

"That's not pride or stubbornness. It's just a fact. He wouldn't want it if I did. He doesn't really want anything. What he needs is a mistress."

"That's not usually the woman's solution."

"Maybe it isn't, but it's true. I have my own center and most of the time I can draw into it when I need to. That's just luck, I guess. Some people have it and some people don't. But if someone hasn't got it, and it isn't supplied from the outside, he has a hard time."

"Still, a mistress? That's something a wife isn't supposed to be able even to say, let alone live with."

"I didn't say it would be easy to live with. Only that it would work. As a matter of fact, I know what my biggest problem would be. If he did have one, I'd have to fight the temptation to become friends with her, to take her over—to disarm him that way too. The hard thing would be for me to leave him free, to keep my hands, my mind, my will completely off the subject. And I could do it. I'm not really castrative, to use that stupid word. If he just once got past having to compare himself to me, he'd find that out. It would work."

"It's tricky, though. American men aren't very good at saving their marriages by means of affairs. The minute they get involved in the quagmire of romance, they assume it's time to bolt out of the marriage into a second. The most likely prospect is that you'd get left."

"It would still be better for him, even if it came to that. He's under a curse of inaction."

"You know something? You have a knack of saying things that sound totally dubious, but when I try to argue them down, they turn out to be unassailable. Not welcome, or pleasant, or even wise. Just unassailable. I can only say 'You're probably right' and then think, 'God help us all.' We really are trapped in our characters."

"I guess so."

"Let's have another round of drinks and order. At least we can make the trap pleasant."

The waitress came. Small debate over what to have. Choice narrowed to fish, then to grilled sole or striped bass Greek style—then to sole by a lifting of the waitress's eyebrow at the mention of the striped bass. He smiled, bowed a silent thank-you to her, and ordered sole. When she left, he toasted Laura again.

"Saved by the kindness of the help from a fish worse than death. It must be pretty grim if onions, tomatoes, oregano and ouzo can't arm-wrestle it into submission."

"See? Your unconscious style pays off. You've made a

conspirator of her. It's very physical, you know. You don't do it just with your eyes like most people. It's your hands, your head, the way you lean back to one side. And I've decided it's not all that unconscious. Second nature is more like it. You don't think about it but you're aware of it."

"No comment. If I opened my mouth, you'd probably X-ray my teeth for good measure. Change the subject."

She thought for a moment, then smiled.

"All right. Romance."

He drew himself up and tilted his head slightly.

"Romance?"

"Yes. Romance. Why is it a quagmire?"

"Who said that?"

"You did. Not five minutes ago. You sounded . . . well, cynical. Is that too strong?"

"A little, I think. The right word is probably 'Sadder, Budweiser.' You know the limerick?"

"Yes. Just tell me about the quagmire."

"You really want to listen to theories?"

"It's better than waiting till September."

"Okay, but don't say I didn't warn you." He picked up a breadstick and held it like a piece of chalk. "The first thing you have to understand is that Romantic Love is not human. It's angelic. Human beings may think it up, but once it gets thought, it acquires a life of its own. It becomes a kind of purely spiritual Power—an Angel—that's fundamentally unsympathetic to flesh and blood. We sit around down here in our warm, furry bodies with all kinds of more or less manageable urges like sex, infatuation, affection, even love, but somehow we're never content. We insist on asking in this Principality, this Dominion called Romance. It's gorgeous, of course—just like the other Angels we've invented: the State, Marriage, Family,

Justice, Art. But they're all aliens. They play by rules we can't live up to in the long run.

"And therefore, if you live long enough, you find out two things. The first is that the likes of us can't make any peace with the likes of them. They steadfastly refuse to become either pets or friends. We invite them in on nights of wisteria and moonlight, but their demands smell like iron and fire in the end. They damn you no matter what. If you leave your wife for your love, you offend the Angel of Marriage. If you try to have your love without leaving, you welsh on the Angel of Romance. Either way, they win and you lose.

"But the second thing you learn is that, in spite of it all, we never seriously think of giving up on them. Cynicism is just a temporary shelter. It lasts only as long as you have enough pain to keep your unbelief going. And the pain lasts only until somebody comes along who can make you forget it. Then, it's Angel time all over again. We're just sitting ducks, waiting for the vision to return."

The waitress brought the food. Laura ate a mouthful of fish and put down her fork.

"You really think nobody lives up to them? Not even for a while?"

"That's the catch. You can say we live up to them for a while, but they don't deal in whiles. Their demands are eternal. Even claptrap love poetry gets that much straight. In their terms, eventual failure is utter failure, in spite of all the glory of the temporary success. The romantic commitment is forever. The marriage vow is till death. Anybody who tries to monkey with that doesn't know what he's dealing with. The hell of it all is simply that there can never be any accommodation between their eternity and our temporality. To recreate them in the image of our failure is to destroy the beauty we love. To leave them in their beauty is to guarantee that sooner or later, we will never do anything but fail."

"You sound as if you've been through something grim."

"No grimmer than most, I guess. It really is a universal trap. The beauty of it calls to you, but you can't do it justice. And that's where the worst part comes in. In the end, Romance just can't deal with failure. We sleep, we forget, we overlook, we forgive. We even help. A drink. The loan of a car. A hug. We can fail each other and still not insist on failure as the last word. But nobody gets away with letting the Angels down. They have no mercy. They never offer you a whiskey. The one who fails must never be hugged again while the world lasts. The Principalities and Powers we live by can't forgive, and we can't live without forgiveness. Catch-22. Q.E.D."

They ate for a while without talking. Finally she spoke.

"There is such a thing as the tyranny of the Angels, you know."

"How do you mean?"

"They refuse to be our pets, but we can also refuse to be theirs. Everything you say is true, except you've got it put together wrong. Or you just haven't got it put together. You have to start where you are."

"Where's that?"

"At the warm, furry body. That's what we are. Human, not angelic. Do you know the poem by Auden?

Lay your sleeping head, my love,
Human on my faithless arm;
...in my arms till break of day
Let the living creature lie
Mortal, guilty, but to me
The entirely beautiful....

She looked straight at him. "I don't care how beautiful the Principalities are. They're not us. We have our own beauty, and they mustn't be allowed to trample it. Not in the name of anything. Not even God."

"How do you stop them?"

"Well, if you find yourself living by something that can't forgive . . ."

She sat silent. Finally she reached out, drew his hand toward her, flashed a smile and said, very rapidly, "then you die to it and look around for something that can."

He held her hand and said nothing.

There is an exigency of time in these matters. Five seconds of holding hands at such a point leaves all the options open; a grateful pat, a resumption of the discussion, a change of subject, an evasion of the issue. Ten seconds introduces a note of doubt—something must be done, but what? Fifteen, and nothing seems possible but continued silence. Twenty, the first hint that whatever must be done is already in the works. Thirty, that it is several sizes larger than anything we had in mind; and, somewhere between thirty and forty, the inevitable ratification of it all by the oldest device known to man: the naming of names.

"Paul . . ."

"Laura . . ."

She let another silence go by. "Forget the pain. It's dead."

He turned his wrist to see his watch. "Just like that? Between noon and . . . one?"

"Just like that . . . between noon and one." She smiled again. "Say 'Us.'"

"Us?"

"Say it without the question mark."

"Us."

"Good. I love you, Paul."

"Laura . . . God! I never thought . . ."

"Then don't think."

He smiled, shook his head and, after a long while, drew her hand to him and kissed it.

"I'll be damned. This has got to be the East Coast record for quiet devastation. What happens now?"

"Just dessert, I guess. I have my period."

*  *  *

(By the way. If you laughed, or smiled, or even felt the least twinge of satisfaction at Laura's last remark, you and I have further to go before we understand each other. Your smirk of appreciation suggests, quite falsely, that the universe can be expected to resolve the dilemma of our freedom by interfering like a mother-in-law in our plans for the season—that the cosmos has an interest in our choices which will protect us from the danger of choosing our interests. I meant nothing of the kind. Any interest that cannot brook four or five days' dull delay is of no interest at all. Laura just had her period. It is no excuse for an attack of the metaphysical heebie-jeebies.)

# 3

When the waitress came back with the change at the end of the meal, Paul figured the tip, pulled two dollar bills off the plate, stuffed one into his tobacco pouch, and handed Laura the other.

"A souvenir."

"That's nice."

She picked up her cigarettes and started to throw them into her shoulder bag. He held up an admonitory forefinger, reached over, took the pack from her hand, and extracted the matches from under the cellophane.

"What are you doing? I always take restaurant matchbooks."

"Not any more, you don't. Stick to the supermarket jobs. Tomato paste ads keep things quieter on the home front."

She took back the cigarettes, shook her head smilingly, and plopped them into the bag.

"There. Clean."

"Good. Now, where's your car?"

"Out in back. But I have to make a stop first."

"It's on the way out. C'mon, I'll show you."

He followed her, guiding her with his hand. When they reached the hall, he came alongside, put his arm around her waist, and drew her to him while they walked. She pressed her hip against his without breaking stride and turned her face up to him. He kissed her lightly, on unparted lips.

Chasteness is always the biggest surprise. We are so inured to the conventions of torrid lovemaking that we forget how many light years love can travel on physical understatement. The ham-handed explicitness of the sexual behavior generally held up for our edification seems to be little more than a frantic checking out of the equipment to see if it's still in working order, a conjuring act to keep away the fear of failure. Our years of sheeplike imitation of it, in marriage or out, leave us unprepared for the day on which the need for conjuring never arises and the thought of failure is impossible. Sex, as we have been taught to think of it, is probably the stupidest of all twentieth century's contributions to the demise of humanity. To have isolated, as a tricky and problematical study in itself, that which is only the reflux, the refulgence of something so grandly certain as to bring tears of laughter . . . Oh, well.

Paul used the men's room while he waited for her. It is a lesser but no less real surprise to be alone for the first time after a declaration of love. Necessarily, in a case like his, the first note struck is always something like, "What the hell have I done now?" But that is only a last reflex stab at Putting It All Together, the final gasp of an integrative habit left over from the days when he had no company in his solitude and could spend his quiet times thinking about himself. Now however, midway between urinal and washstand, he finds his solitude so full of her as to absolve him from further effort to make things jibe. He observes, no doubt, that according to the received wisdom of the race, nothing is supposed to be capable of doing that. The observation, however, is so detached as to be meaningless. This is now a sovereign solitude. Not one into which he retreats in order to balance his books or hide from his creditors; one, rather, to which he goes gladly because she has taken up residence in it. The lover, when he drives alone, drives with the radio off. Washrooms, waitingrooms—all the classical locuses of mindless boredom or fretful reckoning—become for him places of assignation instead. The beloved's name is called to leopard-print walls and black Spanish tile floors. In a perfectly normal conversational voice Paul said, "Laura, I love you." He dried his hands, smiled at himself in the mirror and said, still aloud, but more slowly, "And that . . . said John . . . is that."

He waited for her in the deserted back foyer of the restaurant. When she came out, he took her in his arms and they kissed—once again, gently, chastely. He held her face in his hands.

"You smell good."

"That's Charlie."

"That's only one layer. The second is cigarettes and Drambuie. And the third is the base of your nose: oysters; the wind across a salt marsh."

"All that?"

"More. Your hair is something else. A closed bedroom in an old frame house on a warm afternoon."

"You're making that up."

"Not really. I have a nose with a long memory, and you are a symposium, a convivium of redolences. The only thing I find missing is liver and onions. The single flaw. The base line from which the greatness of the achievement can be measured."

"I love you."

"Seriously, I love your smell. People can think they're

in love, but if they can't stand to breathe each other in, they'll never bring it off."

"I like that. It proves I was right about your being physical. Another validation."

"Of course."

"Of course."

They walked out the rear entrance and over to her yellow Volvo. She unlocked the door, and he drew her to him again, his hands dropping from her waist to the ungirdled roundness of her.

"Nice."

"Nice."

He looked at his watch and patted her on the backside.

"Don't do that."

"Do what?"

"Look at your watch and pat me. That says 'Toddle off.' Pat all you like, but don't do it to telegraph your goodbyes."

"All right. Never again. To hear is to obey. I am your liege man of life and limb. Am I forgiven?"

"You're forgiven."

"Hey, you know what's going through my head? Something from Auden—the *Horae Canonicae,* I think—

Nothing is with me now but a sound,
  A heart's rhythm, a sense of stars
Leisurely walking around, and both
  Talk a language of motion
  I can measure but not read . . .

I can't remember what comes next, but eventually he gets to a line where he says that the constellations 'sing of some hilarity beyond all liking and happening.' I don't know—it just seems to fit. I'll look it up for you. Another souvenir."

"Good."

"Seriously, though, I have to get back."

She said, "All right," kissed him, and slid behind the wheel of her car.

"You leave first, Paul. I want to watch you walk."

At the corner of the restaurant he turned and waved. By the time he got his car started the Volvo was already out on the highway, headed east.

*     *     *

Back at his office Paul found a folded note tucked between the door and the jamb. He went inside, opened the blinds, and read it standing in front of the window.

"Paul. I waited till 3:00. Sorry (?) I missed you. This makes twice. —J."

He looked at his watch: 3:30.

"Damn!"

Downstairs and outside once again. Fast walk to the classroom building where the 4:00 graduate poetry seminar was held. Irving Schiffmann was already there talking to a couple of students.

"Irv. How're you doing?"

"With a two-hour seminar on Monday afternoon? Bloody but unbowed is the best I can tell you. What can I do for you?"

"Has Janet Grigson been by here yet? There's something I'm supposed to give her."

One of the students spoke up.

"She was here just a minute ago. That's her stuff on the table."

Paul headed for the door.

"Thanks. I'll catch her outside. See you, Irv. Sorry to interrupt."

"If you're really sorry, take this seminar for me."

"No way. See you."

He went out into the corridor, walked slowly toward the women's washroom, passed by it to the far end of the hall and leaned against the window. Four minutes.

She came out and headed for the seminar room. Designer jeans. Heels. Turtleneck top.

"Janet."

Quick turn of her head, but no break in stride.

"Wait. Please."

He caught up with her and cut her off.

"Listen. I'm sorry about missing you, but I really did think we said Tuesday. I just got back from lunch. When I got your note, I figured I'd have time to catch you before 4:00, so I came over."

She kept her eyes down. Flushed cheeks. Hair tied back severely.

"Look, Paul. This is no time to talk. Frankly, I'm angry."

"I know. And I really am sorry about it. Last week and this. You free tomorrow?"

"It isn't just two missed dates, Paul. I've been getting funny signals from you for months."

"Don't be like that, love, I'm still around. Nothing's changed."

She looked up at him.

"Don't *you* be like that. That's the whole trouble. You're just around. And not even that, sometimes. Who was the lunch with—male or female?"

"That's got nothing to do with it. It's no skin off your nose."

"Your wife?"

"No, Sarah's in New York today."

"Paul, I don't know how to figure you. You're very sweet and you're marvelous in bed, but I can't take your disappearing act anymore. You've got a head full of little compartments and you keep the people in your life locked in them. Maybe your wife is happy with the visitation schedule you've worked out for her cell, but I'm not happy with mine. You just vanish too often. And I don't mean only broken dates. I mean *you* vanish."

"Look. I'm sorry. I really did think we said Tuesday."

"You said that already. The trouble with you is you're not listening to what I'm saying. I don't know if it's that you won't or that you can't. All I know is that I can't take it any more. If it makes you feel any better, it's not that I don't love you; it's just that I can't cope with you. Maybe your marriage really is great. If it is, that's nice for you. But mine isn't, and I can't handle any more destructiveness than I already have. Let me go. I have to get to class."

"Let me call you tomorrow."

"Oh, Paul, Paul."

"Janet. Come on."

"Paul, I had a friend who used to say that when a conversation got to the point at which two people were simply saying each other's names, they were either busy making love, or they had sunk so deep in misunderstanding that there was no use going on. This is the second."

He reached out his hand and touched her cheek.

"Is it really that bad?"

"I don't want to talk any more. Please. Let me go. This isn't talking anyway."

He tried to meet her eyes, but she kept them down.

"All right, love, I'll see you."
She walked to the classroom without looking back.

*　　　　　*　　　　　*

In fairness—if there is any such thing as fairness in these matters—it should be said that women found it easy to fall in love with Paul. If it was true that his behavior toward them could be described by the unsympathetic as predatory, it was also true that, for as long as his lovers' sympathies held up, they made little effort to avoid him. Especially the ones who, like him, were emphatic and volatile sexual presences. Such people simply recognize each other and close in; sour questions about who did what to whom occur only later on, when the sad, bitchy days begin. For as long as the volatility is in charge, no one is to blame. By the same token, however, no one is particularly responsible either. The timing of romances thus gladly and mutually provoked is seldom convenient. They obtrude themselves not only on marriages, but also on other, and previous, romances. Sometimes before any time has elapsed to allow them to become decently previous. In Paul's life his relationships with women tended to overlap rather than to succeed each other. Love as a many-layered thing. The romantic hero as juggler: one in the bed and two in the air, all night, all month, all year.

Physically he was simply good-looking: trim, six-foot-two, black curly hair conservatively cut, olive skin. Forehead a little too short for handsomeness, but the face cleanshaven, with a cleft chin, full lips, and deepset dark brown eyes. Bedroom eyes. The hack phrase is precise: if he had a single obviously sexual set of physical characteristics it was the lights thrown off by his eyes even behind the glasses he wore for reading and the way the lines at their corners gave the impression of a collusive smile even when his mouth was in repose.

His overall sexual charm, however, sprang from a self-deprecating, sometimes self-mocking manner—and from a gentleness that hinted at some vulnerability waiting to be hunted out. Janet's "you're very sweet" caught it accurately, if grudgingly, but her exasperation at his "vanishing" just as accurately caught the catch in it: the vulnerability was hidden better than anyone suspected at first. Paul was easy to get to, but almost impossible to get at. The sweetness that provoked the instinct of the huntress was itself the lair in which he avoided discovery.

Women frequently lost patience with him, of course, and some actually broke up with him. He, however, never instituted the breaks. He felt himself capable of going on with anything he started. As he saw it, the defalcations came from other hands than his. Only once, and that only in the last year, did a woman ever learn enough about him—penetrate sufficiently the devices of his hiding—to enable her anger to attack the sweetness itself as dishonest and manipulative, and to leave him flat because of it. That was Catharine. And sadly enough, but not so oddly, she had mattered most of all. The painful invitation to self-knowledge had been delivered in the one Dear John letter he was least able to bear.

Most of the rest, however, simply became confused by the impenetrability. If they broke with him at all, it was not because they understood what they were up against, but only because like Janet they finally decided they just couldn't cope. Such breaks, though, had a way of turning out to be impermanent: the ability to cope was eventually refreshed; the angry resolve to stay away from him, unnourished by any clear perception of injustice, withered; and the volatilities simply hung around waiting for another chance—which they often enough got, and used, with their customary disregard for the proprieties of timing. The overlapping got worse instead of better. He juggled more but enjoyed it less and, for the first year in his life, wondered seriously whether he had the strength to keep it up. On good days, and there were many of them, he was his old self; but on the grim ones, he was a man playing out a bad hand at bridge. He had losers he couldn't slough, and he had thrown away his lead to the winning suit. It was just a matter of time till they bled him dry.

It is tempting, of course, to become clinical about these things—to jump to the possibly correct conclusion that he really didn't like women after all and that the qualities by which he attracted them were, subconsciously, the weapons of a vendetta. Unless you are a disinterested psychologist, however, or a patient with five years' worth of money and a clutch of lovers so longsuffering as to hold off foreclosure while you work your way to wholeness, thinking about a clinical cure for misogyny is like standing on a wind-whipped cornice at the twentieth floor and wondering whether you should see a psychiatrist about your acrophobia. There just isn't time. The facts are simply contrary to the conditions of the cure.

And it is just as idle to moralize. Morality helps most when it has the least to object to. If it is a guide at all, it is a guide to the perfecting of one's virtues, not to the reform of one's vices. It keeps nongamblers from being foolish at the racetrack. It does not keep child abusers from beating children, compulsive liars from lying, or lechers from leching. For those in the front trenches of their faults, it is just a lovely, cruel vision of a home they cannot get to. Life, at their extremity, is luck or lumps. The law only makes sin exceeding sinful; it never saved anybody who really needed help.

There is, of course, grace. But grace, besides being unclinical and nonmoral, is also, for someone in Paul's position, unimaginable beforehand and terrifying when offered. It is also, to be sure, curative. But that is the most unimaginable and terrifying thing of all:

> 'Twas grace that taught my heart to fear,
> And grace my fears relieved . . .

Always, unfortunately, in that order.

But while the subject was now ready for him, Paul was, so far at least, not ready for the subject. As he saw it, all he was doing was dropping cards on other people's tricks. The lesson being taught was not grace; it was a graduate course in what it feels like to have all the leads in somebody else's hand. *Inexorability 321.*

*     *     *

He walked back to his office, put his feet on the desk, and stared at the ceiling.

The texture of his new-found solitude, so silken not an hour ago, was coarser than he expected, Laura's sovereignty over it sharper, more steely. He was still her liege man, and gladly; but for the first time he took note of the possible jeopardy of life and limb. Not that he immediately perceived it in depth. At the start, only his body took it in: the skin at the back of his neck tingled; he almost, but not quite, shivered. His mind was busy weighing plausibilities. If Janet wanted out, let her out. The attractiveness of at least that much of a simplification of his life struck him with all the more force because, for once, he found himself contemplating it as a possibility he wanted to encourage rather than as an eventuality that would probably dally forever in coming.

Even intellectually, however, the contemplation flushed some distressing propositions. First, that he knew himself well enough to know that if Janet, alas not impossibly, ever decided she wanted back in, he would most likely just say yes and drop into the old pattern. Second, that a simplification which consisted of reducing the number of concurrent liaisons from five and a half to four and a half while at the same time starting a roaring love affair with Laura was a distinctly bush-league simplification. Third, that the number of people who would be happy with it, himself included, was probably zero. Fourth, that it was practically certain not to simplify anything, but to complicate everything. He played with the words for a while. Simplicate and complify. Why not? But either way, no simplexity. Only complicity.

Fifth and finally, though, he knew he was trapped by Laura no matter what. In less than a minute he had come skipping back across the supposedly unbridgeable gulf that the disastrous end of the affair with Catharine had put between him and romance. The self-protective armor of his luncheon discourse on the impossibility of living with the Dominions, Principalities and Powers had gone whistling down the wind like so many feathers. He was not even a sitting duck; he was a plucked one. The speech might as well have been delivered by another man in another century. The law of the exclusivity of the romantic attachment, so recently and so clearly seen as the murderous infeasibility it was, had been blithely reinvoked as the law of life it could never be for the likes of him. He knew he had to give himself only to Laura, and he knew he couldn't do it. The avenging Angel had been invited in for tea.

There is a reek of death that hangs around the law of life; and Paul sensed it all the more clearly because there had been a time when he didn't smell it at all. He was alive without the law once. For the ten years of the affair with Catharine, he had been simply and happily beyond its jurisdiction. In the first years, his only sin against the Angel of Romance consisted in his continuing to make love to his wife. But there were so many good reasons for that—kindness, fairness, responsibility—that they effectively dispensed him from compliance with the law, even though he had, in principle, invoked it.

As the affair went on, though, other offenses against the Angel began to accumulate. He made love not simply to the wife of his youth and the lady of his heart, but to an impressive number of the English Department's brightest and best. However, since good reasons for these infractions did not come as easily to hand, he was forced to deal with them by constructing the compartments to which Janet referred. He made them law-tight and hid in them safely: either what he did with the others was not what he did with Catharine; or if it was, it did not mean the same thing; or if it became obvious that the others thought it did, he still knew in his heart of hearts that it simply could not. In any case, he managed to make himself on all counts not only above the law in practice but, even better, metaphysically immune to its demands. He had only one love. He really believed that. And it was true. He really did.

The only trouble with such casuistry, however, is that it cannot successfully be explained to anyone else. Because while we can all convince ourselves of its validity on the rough-and-ready level of our furtive bodies and scrawling, misspelt minds—while we can indeed believe we love only one and still have affairs with any number we find convenient and/or possible (it is done day in and night out, probably not too many doors from where you are now so comfortably and domestically seated)—we also know that the human race has tacitly agreed that it's not supposed to be that way once you've invited in the Angel.

Therefore (let us give Paul short and merciful shrift) when, in the last years of his grand passion, the fragments shored against his ruin began, one by one, to wash out—when the day came on which there were no words left that had been spoken only to Catharine, no remaining venereal acts that had not been essayed with at least one other Venus—he began to wonder just what, if anything, he still believed in his heart of hearts.

The upshot of it, of course, was that in his effort to regain his faith in himself—in his panic to render credible once again the largeness of the love that was his life—he did the one thing that was simply and absolutely undoable: he told Catharine the truth. Having offended the Angel, he proved his worthiness as a knight of romance by conceding the law's dominion over him and confessing his offenses against it. To which the Angel, as anyone with his wits about him would have known, replied, "That is one hell of a note," and slammed the door in his face. He invoked the law, which was just, holy and good, and quite properly got the only sentence possible: sin revived, and he died. And that also is true. He really did. First, tears. Then terror. Then the coldness of the grave.

But now. Damn, damn, *damn!* To begin to try to live

again. To raise the dead only to the certainty of a second death. To submit once again to the inexorability of romance and thus revive the exceeding sinfulness of his inevitable faithlessness. To turn into unpardonable offenses against a new sovereign lady those unendable liaisons which, since Catharine left, had at least seemed more like penances than vice. To put himself so irrevocably on the path to some bed, someday, where he would slip and say to Laura, "Oh, Cath." To know all that, and to be able to do nothing but wait in the cold light of that knowledge for the ax to fall. Stupid, stupid.

But, of course, it was all irrevocable. Finished, too late, no way back. Best, perhaps, not even to think of it. Play out the hand. Hope that the compartments can somehow be made to hold. Is that irresponsible? Who's to say? If you're going to gyp everybody in the end, what's the rush to go running around insisting on gypping them sooner rather than later? Impossible promises, badly kept, are still promises kept as best you can. Maybe, with luck . . .

He put his feet down, locked up the office, got in his car, and drove aimlessly for ten minutes. Then he headed for the restaurant, circled once through the parking lot, and went on toward home.

"Laura. Laura. Laura."

# 4

At this point it may be instructive to put Paul's problem in its proper, larger context. Romance being simply a
special case of the angelic generality called law, perhaps
we can best understand the shipwreck of his love life—
and the prospects of the salvage operation so diffidently
just begun—by taking a somewhat idiosyncratic look at
one of the classic texts on law and grace: Proposition XIII,
from Augustine's *Exposition of Certain Propositions from
the Epistle to the Romans*.

I shall gloss the passage for you in the grand old manner. As I see it, the only major liberty I take with the text
is my substitution of *romance* for *law* every time the latter
occurs. Aside from that I consider my reading to be thor-
oughly consonant with the letter of Augustine, as well as
distinctly redolent of the spirit of Luther—and, therefore,
irreproachably both Catholic and Reformed. But judge for
yourself.

\*         \*         \*

In his exposition of Romans 3:20 ("Therefore no flesh
is justified before him by *romance:* for by *romance* comes
the knowledge of sin") Augustine points out that there
will always be certain dummies floating around who will
interpret such remarks as a crack at *romance*. He adds,

however, that if such boneheads would only learn to read carefully enough, they would see that neither does the Apostle take a dim view of *romance* nor is the free will of man taken from him and hauled off to the cosmic garbage heap. The general mess we find ourselves in, he feels, will not yield to such lamebrained attempts to clean it up.

He suggests, accordingly, that we distinguish carefully the four necessary steps or stages by which we pass from our fallen state to the fully human condition. He lists them as:

before *romance,*
under *romance,*
under grace, and
in peace;

and he construes them as follows.

Before *romance,* he says, we go tearing around, rolling back the lid of the sardine can of life, and acting, in general, as if we had a metaphysical right to the full fruition of every luscious desire that occurs to us. Under *romance,* however, the condition is reversed: we are dragged about, willy-nilly and without ceremony, by our commitment to what now seems like nothing but a bevy of well-muscled beauties who no longer care a fig for our discomfort and who stop their ears at anything that pleads, however sweetly, for our undistress. Under grace, though, things are better: we neither pursue the riot of desires, nor are we bullied about by it. And finally, in peace, securely under the mercy, the riot simply stops: the wolf and his lambs (Laura, Sarah, Catharine, Janet, et al.) dwell together in gardens and gallant walks; the leopard lies down on an eschatological bed of green with all the kids he has ever pursued, the sucking child plays upon the hole of the asp, and they neither hurt nor destroy in all my holy mountain, saith the Lord.

Augustine then continues. *Before romance,* he says, it's all tea and cake: we not only desire incompatibilities and gobble indigestibilities, but we actually get away with it all, our hearts unhaunted by any fear of judgment and our minds sustained by an unshakeable conviction that it's the greatest thing since sliced bread.

However, once we have, by the tough luck of our better nature, acknowledged ourselves to be *under romance*—once we have taken the lovely, deadly vow to put our nose between the Angel's teeth and hang on tight—we have a fight on our hands. But then, alas, far from finding it a fair fight, let alone one from which we might hope to go forth conquering and to conquer, we find to our deep pain and abiding sadness that we are, at every hour of the day and night and with no time off for good behavior, consistently having the living daylights pounded out of us by none other than the referee we ourselves picked for the match. . . .

Which, if it is not a happy place to leave off this exposition of Augustine, is still a suitable one. We are at least reassured: we have arrived, by a consideration of Scripture and the Fathers, at the very point to which Paul got himself by staring at the ceiling. We have, of course, considerably further to go; for now, however, it is a comfort to have struck a trial balance.

# 5

Paul himself, however, did not remain long at the balance point. The ten minutes of aimless driving, plus the nostalgic swing through the restaurant parking lot, obliterated the boding negativism of his office meditation and switched him onto automatic pilot for the conduct of an affair. It was, of course, a device with which he was familiar; and if you have even the least knowledge of how it works, you know perfectly well what happened next. He passed a pay phone, checked his watch (4:55), stopped at the next booth he came to, looked up Laura's number, and dialed it. (He also memorized it—deliberately, but passing no particular judgment in the process. No matter that he already had a whole catechism of numbers learned by heart; it was simply convenient that he now learn this one—merely unavoidable that the romantic ratchet should thus inch another step forward and the pragmatic pawl snap into place behind it.)

The phone rang. Laura and a child picked up the two extensions simultaneously.

"Laura?"

"It's all right Jimmy. It's for me. Hang up."

Paul waited for the click.

"Are you able to talk for a minute?"

"Hold on."

She set down the phone, closed the door, and came back.

"Now I am. I'm upstairs in the bedroom. I was just thinking of you."

"Likewise. Obviously. I love you."

"I would have died if you hadn't called."

By another reflex action of his mind, he noted one more pull of the ratchet, one more click of the pawl.

"So would I. Listen. Is there any chance I can see you tomorrow? I'm tied up with classes and conferences till about 1:00, and I have to drive up to the Catskills for a dumb conference that starts with supper, but I can get free for a while in the early afternoon. Can I meet you somewhere? Even if it's only for a few minutes. I just want to see you again."

"So do I. But a conference? You didn't say anything about that. When will you be back?"

"Thursday afternoon late."

"Paul! That's forever."

"I know. That's my second reason for calling. Can you meet me for lunch on Friday?"

"Of course. Give me a minute to think about tomorrow though."

She was silent for a while.

"I have to be at Jimmy's school at 3:00, but before then is all right."

"Good. I really should be on my way be 2:30 anyhow."

"Where should I meet you?"

He hesitated only a second.

"You know the Hill's shopping plaza about a mile past the restaurant?"

"Yes."

"Well, suppose I meet you there at the far end of the parking lot at 1:30?"

"You mean the west end?"

"Hey, you really are amazing. You're not only punctual, you actually know east from west."

"I'm just a born girl scout."

"You're a lot more than that. But you can come then? I mean, it's not going to be too much of a hassle?"

"If I'm not there, it won't be my fault."

"Good. 1:30. Hill's Plaza. West end. Right now, though, I have to run and liberate the babysitter before she pauperizes me. Sarah won't be back till after supper. I love you."

"I love you."

*     *     *

They wound down over the next minute in an alternation of endearments and a series of hesitations over who should hang up first. I spare you those. Pillow talk, even on real pillows, makes dull reading. Transcribed from phone conversations, it is a sovereign soporific.

You may wonder, however, why I have said so little about Laura's and Paul's relationships to their respective spouses. There are two reasons. The first is that it is not to my purpose to do so. I am not developing here either a full-fledged cast of characters or a convoluted plot. My intention is simply to isolate a single moment in the relationship between two lovers; I shall give you only as much of its wider context as is necessary to that end. I am convinced, as I said at the outset, that to introduce any more than a little of the tissue of their lives would cause your mind to cast such a moral pall over the narrative that it would distract you from the vision of grace.

The second reason, however, is that in an affair of this sort, where people are not playing conventional matrimonial guilt games—where they are not perpetually canvassing each other on the subject of fidelity in order to expiate whatever it is they think they have left undone at home—there is a tacit agreement that the names of the spouses involved should come up only in a moderate and neutral way, that they should be neither completely suppressed nor extensively discussed. I state this simply as a fact: it just happens that some people do make such a decision. I pass no particularly favorable—or unfavorable—judgment upon it.

In the case at hand, Paul and Laura arrived at the decision by similar routes, but for slightly different reasons. They were both convinced their partners were not about to bolt: Paul, because he thought his wife was genuinely pleased with the tenor of their life; Laura, because she felt that, while her husband was frequently displeased with their marriage, he was not about to be seriously enough interested in anything else to make a break. Needless to say, they were both right and both wrong. They had the insights and the blind spots of strong characters—of the kind of people who cause, rather than experience, jealousy.

They were right about discounting any strong possibility of action against them: Paul, because he was as graciously private from his wife as from anyone else and so gave her anger no provable inequities to feed on; Laura, because her husband had been jealous without cause for so many years that he simply had no faculty left for satisfying himself as to the difference between a real wolf and an imagined one. They were wrong, though, in that they underestimated the potential vehemence of the objections they themselves so easily dismissed. The infirm, imperfect jealousies they aroused seemed to them a kind of vindication; in reality, however, their spouses were frequently more upset at their own inability to justify their envy than they were at the objects of it. Those who are stymied have, in the very fact of their being boxed, a taproot to their anger that is almost always overlooked by those who box them. People who stymie others are never as safe as they think they are.

In any case, however, it is all irrelevant. In spite of the dangers, nothing happened. Nor was there any reason to expect that it should have. Affairs, while they are commonly thought of as being conducted in the interstices of lives, are not the inevitable problem the imagery suggests. There is more room in the cracks of our existence than anywhere else. Lives, like atoms, are in fact mostly interstices. Even the densest of them, the ones so filled with projects and associations as to present a facade of seamless busyness, are full of gaping interstellar distances. The brief, mindless times of the stirring of the breakfast coffee, of the fastening of the seat belt, of the moment alone in the washroom, all open out into vast, silent halls for which no heart's leap or mind's journey will ever be too great.

Romance does not, except in the hands of fools, necessarily attack what already exists in a life, any more than the tide has to uproot the marsh grasses in order to rise. Love and water flow around obstacles and, in flood, are just as likely to nourish roots as tear them out. That is not a wish. It is simply the way things are, given half a chance. The lover sings in the shower, pats his dog, and is generally a pleasure to be around. The beloved's complexion improves.

You need bold souls to bring it off, of course. It can't be accomplished by a pair of enamored fussbudgets continually trimming their sails to every mean-spirited wind they meet; but it can be done and it has been done, and that is that. Don't let the false notion that the cosmic vice squad is on twenty-four-hour duty lead you into the even falser expectation that everyone who breaks the received rules will be hauled in and fined. Until you see that we get something both far better and far worse than that, you won't see grace at all.

So accept for now Paul's and Laura's luck and wish them well. If it comforts you, your sacred conviction that there is no such thing as a free lunch is still true—and in a more terrible and wonderful sense than you have yet understood. Grace is neither indulgence nor permission. The divine comeuppance is still there. Literally, and with a capital "C."

In the immediate instance, though, Paul and Laura proceeded, without a hitch, to their respective kinds of meal and evening. He, having once turned his mind to the subject of domesticity, did not take the sitter home after all; instead he fed the children, picked up Sarah at the station on the 7:54, and took her to a seafood house for dinner. Laura, after Paul hung up, called a couple to whom she knew her husband was not averse, invited them for drinks around 9:00, and spent the meantime with her husband, her children and Keats, respectively, in the approximate proportions of one part to five parts to two. Paul got to bed at 11:00; Laura at 1:00. Both their evenings were successes. Neither of them—and for the same reasons—made love.

Laura got to the shopping plaza at 1:35, parked right next to his car and said, "My place or yours?"

"Mine," he said, leaning over to open the door. "More room."

When she got inside, there were no words; just a sudden, long kiss in the twisted, half-trapped position dictated by front seats of cars. After a while, Paul reached down and slid the seat back.

"This is ridiculous. Turn around, put your feet up, and lie across my lap."

"Here? In the parking lot?"

"Sure, here. The best hiding place is where nobody expects to find anything hidden. 'The Purloined Letter.' "

He put his left hand on the steering wheel and she laid her head in the crook of his arm.

"That better?"

"Much."

They kissed again. He touched her face with his fingers, outlining her lips, her eyebrows, the line of her jaw. Finally she spoke.

"I read the tarot last night. Yours, mine, and ours."

"Was it good?"

"Very. Another validation. It's all safe."

"You're serious about that aren't you? I mean about the tarot. I've never paid any attention to it except as a literary device. Too much residual scientism in my head, I guess."

Her eyes widened and she lifted her head animatedly.

"But that doesn't have to stop you. I figured out the answer to at least a part of that long ago. It's really just a way of letting your mind . . ."

He waited for her to finish, but she didn't.

"Of letting your mind what?"

"Of letting your mind meditate on certain images. At least, that's one way you can think of it, even if you don't go any further."

"That's still just inside your own head, though. How do you get from there to the conclusion that you and I are all safe?"

She fell silent again, then half sat up and looked straight at him. "Well, for one thing, the images—the cards themselves—are facts. They're not just inside your own head. They're out there on the table, being whatever they are. And of course, if you believe there's anything behind them . . ."

"How do you mean?"

"Like in Charles Williams. *The Greater Trumps.*"

He puzzled for a minute.

"You mean the cards represent forces that actually reach you through the reading?"

"I guess so."

She didn't say anything more, so he tried explaining it himself.

"Well, I can see one way it might work: the cards are representations of actual elements in the experience of the race: the Fool, the Hanged Man, and so on. Those things definitely have power; so, if the cards, as images of them, manage to turn them loose in your mind . . . Hey, listen.

You've not only got me arguing your case, you've got me leaving off the ends of sentences just like you."

"You work too hard to be clear."

"My curse, I guess."

"It's not a curse. But it's not everything either. You have to be more open, that's all. Then it just comes. You interrelate . . ."

He ran his fingers over her forehead.

"You know what? I've figured out how you got tagged as a scatterbrain. Your mind isn't scattered, it's elliptical. It leaves out steps, because it sees where it's going and figures everyone else does too. But your speech is also elliptical, especially at the ends of sentences. Aposiopetic. Unfortunately, it takes more getting used to than most people are prepared for."

"Apo– what?"

"Aposiopetic. Aposiopesis: the trick of trailing off into silence for rhetorical effect. Example: 'But for anyone to have thought that Carter was a genuine threat in 1980 . . .' Your silences aren't that rhetorical, but they have their effect."

"I never thought about it. And I especially never thought about apo– whatever-it-is."

Something bumped the back of the car. She made a sudden move to sit up, but he kissed her before she could.

"It's nothing. Just a couple loading groceries into their trunk. The shopping cart rolled into us."

"How'd you know that?"

"The rear view mirror. I spotted them a minute ago when they walked up. Panic not."

"I like that. Your coolness, I mean."

"What else is there to do? If they don't know you, they will quite intelligently assume you are two lovers

[ 45 ]

having a tryst at a shopping plaza; and, since that is one of the main uses of such places, they will think no more of it than that cigar-smoking old party over there who's been watching ever since you got here.

"If, on the other hand, they do know you, there's always the hope that, in their preoccupation with their own lives, they still won't notice you. However, when a woman not previously visible sits up suddenly in a front seat, straightens her skirt, and arranges her hair . . . Aposiopesis again."

She threw her arms around him and held herself close.

"I love you, I love you, I love you."

*     *     *

They talked for a while about the conference he was going to at Grossinger's, an ad hoc affair pulled together for one measure of serious discussion about the miserable state of the English language among freshmen, three measures of eating and drinking and, depending on individual tastes, an optional number of measures of fun and games on the golf course, in the pool, up and down the corridors, or in the skin bars around Monticello. Apropos of the last, Paul said he wondered whether tractor salesmen in such places pretended to be English teachers, because, in his experience, most English teachers certainly made a point of acting as if they were tractor salesmen.

Laura turned her head toward his chest and buried her face.

"I wish I could go."

"So do I. Maybe someday, who knows?"

He made a point of not looking at his watch.

"What time do you have?"

"You look. I don't want to."

He turned her left wrist toward him.

"I really should go."

"I don't want you to."

"But I still have to."

She buried her face again.

"Laura?"

"I'm being a brat."

She held herself against him for a few seconds more and then sat up, turned herself around on the seat and smiled.

"You have to come and sit in my car for one minute. I can't walk away from you, you know."

*　　　*　　　*

After they parted, he drove up to the conference in high spirits, spending the whole stretch of Route 17 on the prospect of being naked with her. At Grossinger's his behavior was part that of a veteran conference goer and part that of a man in love. He skipped sessions that didn't interest him, called her every day, wished she were at the poolside or in the Pink Elephant Lounge, got roped into an expedition to the joints in Monticello and lay down, happily discontent, in a lonely bed.

He called her again just before he left on Thursday afternoon but got no answer. He tried later, still without success, at several pay phones on the way down. By the time he got through the traffic jam near the City it was suppertime and too late.

# 7

Paul woke at 6:00 on Friday morning in an unexpect
ed state of morbid agitation. He had gone to bed early the
evening before to catch up on the sleep lost at the conference, and he slept heavily until 3:00 A.M. After that, however, the night deteriorated into a series of dream-ridden
naps, the worst of which took him into one of his recur-
rent nightmares about Catharine.

Their principal theme was estrangement, harped on
till his nerves gave out. Sometimes she would be next to
him on the fringes of a party, obviously upset at being
seen with him and constantly trying to get away; at others, he would run into her downtown only to find that she
had a train to catch. In any case he was always an inconvenience. She either flatly refused to speak to him or, if
she condescended, launched into a monologue about the
enormity of his deception. When he pleaded, as he always did, that he had at least eventually told her the
truth, she dismissed the argument out of hand: it was too
little, too late, and for too much. Besides, why was he
wasting his time with her? He still had plenty of other
places to peddle his papers.

He would cry, of course, and swear he loved her, and
ask why she refused to understand; and she would marvel
at his denseness, daring him to tell any of the others what
he had told her and see what would happen. Then his

frustration would boil over into rage, and he would call her a vengeful bitch and swear at her until remorse stopped him with the thought that he had finally gone too far. And then there would be fear, and sadness, and one more desperate attempt to plead his love before she left.

But none of it made any difference. She was pure ice. She would not hold him or touch him. If the dream lasted long enough, she simply turned her back and left him for dead. Once or twice during the past year, the scenario had been different: not a nightmare, but a dream of reconciliation, or of the way it was. But if anything, that was worse. The bad dreams simply confirmed the death of hope; waking from a good one, he had to go through the dying all over again.

He got up, dressed, and went for a walk. About a mile out of the village, he found a spot under some trees at the edge of a field and stretched out on the grass.

Usually he found that watching clouds through the branches disengaged his mind and cut it back to an idle. This time, however, it didn't work. He was locked into seeing Laura at 12:30 for lunch. The clutch was jammed; his mind simply sputtered and backfired its way along.

He first went through a series of revisionist considerations about his new love. Perhaps, like a fool, he had simply gone in over his head in the hope of a revival of what he had with Catharine. What after all did he really know about Laura? Well, for one thing, that she had the kind of intellect he normally gave the widest possible berth: diffuse, mystical, elliptical as hell. How do you prove to the gallery of watchers you carry inside your head that you haven't just bought yourself one more broad with an extra-normal body and a freaky mind? Answer: you don't. Inside your head or out, your enemies won't believe you and your friends—including, especially, yourself—are too confused by the facts to make up their minds. There's no point in evaluating what you've done. The only point is, it's done. If you've made a mistake about her, you've made it, and there's no way out without still more mistakes. Just hold onto your cold feet and shiver quietly.

Anyway, maybe Laura wasn't just a rerun of Catharine. He repented of his revisionism. She was herself and that was enough. Maybe he would be better off with somebody who could say her husband needed a mistress and really mean it, somebody who, finally and thank God, knew east from west and who seemed to do what she damn pleased with no problems except about practicalities. Maybe she really was great, with her "of course's," and her stacked tarot pack, and the easy openness of her moods.

But then he repented of that, too, because it was just a cheap shot at Catharine. Sure, she had backed and filled and bucked and reared the whole time of their affair, but she really had been his life and he had borne it all gladly as a small enough price to pay. It was hypocritical to make comparisons now that he wouldn't have allowed then. He was wrong no matter what he did. There was no way of feeling good about anything. He watched the clouds and tried not to think.

His tongue, however, had found the loose tooth. In spite of the pain of having lost Catharine—and in spite of the ease with which he could still become furious with her for having killed in ten minutes what they had nursed together for ten years—he was finally able, after a year now, to see it from her point of view. On two levels. The first was the level of the woman scorned. He saw at last that the intentions of the scorner didn't matter a damn compared with the feelings of the scornee. Everyone has to live with the gallery of watchers she carries inside her own head. It makes no difference that real watchers, outside the injured mind, would no doubt be more lenient in their judgment as to who had been made a fool of and more accurate in their assessment of just who was the real fool. The fact of the matter was that when the gallery inside cried "fool," the owner of the head had no choice but to take it personally.

But he also saw it from her point of view on a second, more devastating level. The real trouble was himself. His compartmentalized life. His trick of being apparently open but actually closed. His buying of peace with silence, of other people's happiness at the price of integrity.

He railed for a while at the thought of integrity. Bullshit. To take the likes of us, with our half-assed commitments and our two-bit gifts, and to insist on principle that we run around informing every love, however happy, that she is not the only being in the world whom we have called, in a burst of enthusiasm, the greatest thing since the electric pencil sharpener—to ask us to spell out in words of one syllable the fact that our oblation of life and limb so grandiloquently and so personally offered has, alas, a string or two attached and that, at times she will never note on her watch and in places she will never visit, and in ways we know can never compromise the fullness of our gift, she is being somehow shortchanged—to require, in fine, that her lover print a surgeon general's warning on his forehead stating that he is not exactly Jesus Christ himself . . . well, what the hell did she expect? Not even Origen could pass a test like that.

And yet. And yet. You can say bullshit all you like.

You can appeal from the inapplicability of the law until your breath runs out. But Harry, Harry, Harry, you can't abrogate the stupidity by which you first filed this suit you would now so dearly like to drop. Who appealed to Caesar to begin with? You, Paul. Whose idea was it to take a stand on his citizenship in the City of Romance once again? Who rewrapped the two-bit gift and handed it to Laura on the old sterling platter? You, you dummy. You.

The railing stopped. What was the use? The dare still stood: tell somebody—anybody—everything, and see how long you last. He had enough Christianity left to believe that somehow, after all, there was grace. But in the last year he had hedged his bets and said there was no grace except grace itself—that everything else was law and therefore death. Maybe God could deal with honesty; unfortunately no one else could. People asked you in all sincerity to tell them the truth. What they didn't understand was that when they got it, they would have to blow your head off.

And yet. Always, and yet. What was he to do with Laura? How be literally naked with her and still hide? How make her all and then have to treat her as one more part to be kept in ignorance of the other parts? In plain English, how bed her in the grand romantic tradition and still go on making time and place for all the other bedding down that was still, except for Janet—maybe—unavoidable? Answer? No way.

No way except the dare, which was no way. It was only a trick to get you to stick your head up over the parapet. He thought back to Laura at the restaurant: "If you find yourself living by something that can't forgive ..." Hope sprang up in the aposiopesis. The rhetorical ax was laid to the root of the unacceptable tree, but suddenly, dazzlingly, sheathed: "... then die to it and look around for something that can."

But was that even believable? Forgiveness is for bad boys who finally see light at the end of the tunnel: "... for these, and for all my other sins which I cannot now remember, I am very sorry, and firmly purpose amendment ..." What about the poor slobs who couldn't say that if they wanted to, for whom the future will be only a repetition of the unrelieved darkness of the past? What are they supposed to do? Walk in and say, "Darling, forgive me for what I am about to do. I don't really want permission, but I'm afraid that if you and I are going to do business, you'd better sign this hall monitor's pass just in case"? Just try it and see how far you get. There really was no grace except grace, if indeed there was that. The only true filling in of the ellipsis was: "... then die." The rest was pious pap.

And therefore it had been over all along. It was not a matter of waiting for a slip of the tongue to kill him; he had been dead from the beginning. The illusion of life had served only to trick him into telling the truth that was untellable, into walking once more into the confessional where the priest waited with a pistol. It was only sad that, in six hours, the corpse would have to be propped up and shot again.

# 8

Paul dropped off to sleep.

\*       \*       \*

There are people (perhaps you among them; there was a time when even Paul himself was) who think that the kind of internal debate he was going through is simply a large fuss over not much—that all he really needed was a swift kick to get him off the dime of fooling around onto the dollar of commitment. But they are wrong. They are deceived by the imagery of the salutary jolt: the earnest but almost playful nudge administered by an attentive friend to an associate whose mind has momentarily wandered from its purpose. The swift kick, as actually bestowed, is never like that. When it is given by someone who has paid careful attention to the associate for whom it is intended, it is not only swift but fatal. In words of one syllable, Catharine cut him off and let him bleed to death.

On the other hand, when it is administered by the universe—by the passage of time or by the changes and chances of this mortal life—it is seldom swift and almost never attentive. The universe is just as deadly, of course, but it kills us the way a cat kills a cockroach: it stalks us with a distracted implacability, piercing us now with a claw, then chasing its own tail, coming back by and by to crunch us once with its teeth and spit us out in disgust, going off in pursuit of dust kittens, and returning to us only as long as we are alive enough to interest it. It doesn't want our death, really; it is simply that in its mindless amusement with our life, it never leaves until it has finished us off.

But the final reason why the supposedly therapeutic boot never works lies deeper. No refinement of the way it is applied—no gentling of it in the hands of our lovers, no more systematic direction of it in the advances of the cosmic cat—can overcome the intractability of what it aims to reform. Our mind has not momentarily wandered from its purpose; it is a dead horse. Neither love taps nor systematic violence work when you have a corpse on your hands.

Perhaps, however, you think that all this talk of death and corpses is a bit overwrought—that St. Paul is being more rhetorical than factual when he cries out in Romans 7:24, "O wretched man that I am! Who shall deliver me from the body of this death?" After all, you say, no one in such a state is *all* dead. Give him time; there's life in the old boy yet. He'll be back on his feet in a week.

To which I can only say you haven't paid attention to what death is and insist that you sit through a short excursus on the subject.

*    *    *

Death is the separation of body and soul. You do not believe in souls? That is quite all right; neither, I think, do I. At least I have nothing to say about them except in this context. If you like, think "life" when I say "soul" (in Greek, the same word does for both); we are simply casting about for some concept that will fix in our minds the difference between a body and a corpse.

The point is crucial. A body is capable of nutrition, growth, recuperation, locomotion. There is no use feeding corpses or putting Unguentine on their burns. Death, whatever it is, puts an end to the practicability of all that. But note precisely what is involved. Distinguish carefully between death and deadness. Death occurs; deadness slowly catches up with it. One minute after my death has occurred, my corpse will still be teeming with lives. My kidney perhaps or my heart, if otherwise sound, will be quite capable of being transplanted into someone else. Indeed, if you care to be whimsical and endow my heart with an intellect of its own for a moment, you can imagine it frantically phoning the local paper and running a Situation Wanted ad: *Sound heart, low mileage, never driven by anything but beautiful women, desires new life in which to resume unfortunately interrupted projects. Prefer poet or guitarist but will settle for bassoon player.*

Do you see the point? My heart's problem is not that it is dead, but that it is still alive in the midst of death. It is trapped in a corpse instead of a body. Something— indeed, the one and only necessary thing—has walked out on it. That is why "soul" (or some other word that will do the same work) is inevitable. The difference between life and death is the presence or absence of something like an interambient fluid by which the parts of a body communicate with each other, by which they are enabled to coinhere in the whole. Catharine, you see, really was Paul's life, his soul; she was what the beloved always is, an *aqua vitae* filling him, a vivifying cordial that warmed and unified the parcels of his existence. Everybody knows that: the lover sings in the shower and pats his dog. . . . And everybody knows what happens when, by death or desertion, the beloved leaves: shower stall, soap, bath mat, towel, mind, body, furry paws and floppy ears are all still in place, still functioning. But now, not in life but in death. He who was alive and whole has been reduced to the mere sum of his parts. It isn't just that he feels dead; it's that he has entered death itself.

Which is why, when you think about it, St. Paul is quite accurate in his choice of words. He has, in Romans, been trying to pinpoint the essence of our fallen romantic condition, and he has arrived at the concept of Sin with a capital "S." Not sins, not infractions, not intermittent derelictions, not vices: quite sensibly, he sees that they are not the problem; a living lover can have many things wrong with him and still love magnificently. No, he is looking for the heart of the matter, for a word to describe a condition in which even virtue and truth and beauty and intelligence and kindness and love itself somehow can't manage to bring off what they know perfectly well how to do.

So having settled on the concept of Sin, he then proceeds to illuminate his insight by equating it with three other words: with "concupiscence"; with "the flesh"; and with "death." Notice that all three notions have one thing in common: they describe a condition in which the parts are somehow condemned to act in the absence of the whole—in which the most they can do is masquerade as the whole, and in which they frequently do a good deal less than that.

"Concupiscence," or desire (misleadingly, at least for our times, translated as "lust"), refers not to desire properly so-called—not to the natural mechanism by which the appetites of the several parts coinhere to draw the whole to its own proper good—but to the free-for-all of conflicting desires we commonly experience. Not one life-giving love, unifying and edifying, but a wearing, tearing riot of separately gorgeous affections that lead us, six ways for Sunday, by the nose: Laura, Sarah, Janet, Catharine . . .

"The flesh" does the same conceptual work. It refers not to the body as a body, but to the body as mere meat. And meat always comes from a corpse: loin, rib, rump, or shoulder, it is all nothing but parts going their own way because the unifying life has departed from them. They have a certain acceptability only because they are not yet corrupt, but the soul that animated them is gone and by and by corruption will have its perfect work.

And "death"? Well, I have done that one way; let me change the approach slightly.

Imagine with me a scene of utter tranquility—a tidal marsh in the morning sun. No houses, no people; a place ages ago returned to nature—its only record of human occupation, the vestiges of a long-abandoned wharf. Think of it at high tide: fish swim among the ancient pilings, mussels in great black clumps open and close at leisure taking nourishment from the sea water, currents flow among the grasses at the bottom, and the wind textures the surface with a thousand hammerstrokes. The place is a convivium, an ecological whole, a symbioticum, a living thing, a body.

Postulate next, however, a maximum depth at high tide of two feet and a difference between high and low water of three feet. Then imagine the place six hours later: the pilings stand exposed, the mussels are shut tight, and the grasses lie in clumps on the sand. No fish swim, no currents eddy. The water, the interambient, circumambient medium that made the parts a whole is gone. None of the individual elements is any different than it was before; the lives that were there in the morning are still lives now. But the place itself, the convivium that it was, is in death and not in life. Catharine, if you will, has simply drained herself out of it and, unlike the tide, has sworn she won't be back.

Worse yet, some idiot, namely this sleeping Paul himself, has come along and so bulldozed and damned the channel that no water will ever reach him again. The tides will rise and fall everywhere as before and, down to the last dying of the last part of his life, he will sense them and long for them. But for all that, he will never know them. Catharine gone, Laura precluded, he is a drained marsh. His death is accomplished; his history as a living thing is over. For the rest of his existence he will be simply the annalist of his own corruption.

*      *      *

Paul woke, got up from the grass, and walked home mulling over his options. They were, as he saw them, three.

The first was the boldest and most elegant: stand her up. Just don't go to the restaurant at all. For once in your life, do something brave for a change. Stop palming tenth-rate love off on people; when she asks you why and pleads her love, say nothing. Be the bastard you are. Don't apologize, don't explain; just say, "It's over," and make it stick. That was cruel, of course, but it was the least unkind thing in the long run.

It was also, however, impossible. No one does anything of that magnitude for once in his life. We are all, at the core of our self-regard, nice bastards; in the clutches we don't change, we revert to form. He could no more violate his self-image of the gentle, loving man than he could shed his skin. Nor, finally, could he deny either his love for Laura or his longing for the escape from death she so poignantly—if so impossibly—held out to him. He went only thirty paces before her last words at the shopping plaza caught up with him: "I can't walk away from you, you know," and his heart dissolved in an insanity of desire and compassion. His quite praiseworthy wish to see only the briefest, most surgical pain inflicted by his hand went the way of all concupiscent desires: it was just another lovely part of his nature, and it was mugged by all the other parts in the grand, eye-gouging, knee-in-the-groin war in his members—in one of the endemic rumbles between rival street gangs that were the only action left in the ghetto of his being.

The second option was to show up, go on with the affair, and just hope she never found out about his inevitable welshing on her. But that possibility went whistling even faster than the first. It had, in fact, been closed out long ago by his invocation of the law of romance: he really did believe that the impossible commitment was holy, just and good; and, after Catharine, he knew he could never even try to serve it again without being honest. It was the old double bind: by your very delight in the law after the inner man, you are brought into captivity to the law in your members. The faker who has finally come to a noble loathing of his fakery has no choice but to expose himself as a fake.

Which, of course, was the third option: the dare. Tell her the truth and take your chances. Suddenly, oddly, he felt almost cheerful. His mind flitted to a passage from *The Elder Statesman:*

If a man has one person, just one in his life,
To whom he is willing to confess everything—
And that includes, mind you, not only things criminal,

Not only turpitude, meanness and cowardice,
But also situations which are simply ridiculous,
When he has played the fool (as who has not?)—
Then he loves that person, and his love will save him.

For the first time since he had confessed to Catharine, he admitted into his mind the thought of what it might be like to live without the burden of his duplicity. It was as if he had been on an endless forced march with a sixty-pound pack on his back—the kind of situation you eventually become so inured to that you even forget you ever seriously hoped to get out of it—but then someone not clearly friend or foe drives by with an empty truck, stops, and waits for you to catch up. And you think to yourself, "Oh, God; maybe . . ." And all at once, in the moment before the moment of truth, you are stunned by the weight of the doubt, and thrilled by the hope of deliverance, and terrified by the fear of false hope; and you are angry and sick and sad that you have no control over any of it.

But when your case is like Paul's, it is the terror and the sadness that ultimately prevail. Somewhere else in *The Elder Statesman,* Lord Claverton observes that no one confesses where there is no hope of forgiveness. That was true. When he confessed to Catharine, his confession, however long it was in coming, was finally made in the hope—no, that is too bland—it was made in the presumption of forgiveness, a presumption so strong that the confession itself was hardly more than an embarrassment. The thought that absolution might be withheld never occured to him: he knew he would be forgiven out of love. But he wasn't, and the shipwreck of that certainty had become the governing experience in his mind. In thinking of confessing to Laura, therefore, he could find no knowable reason for doing it. All he knew was that, barring some miracle of indifference or inattentiveness in her—some bizarre turning of a tin ear to his cacaphony, some defect of mind that would tolerate the standing of all known values on their heads—he would simply be condemned again.

Still what else was there? Maybe, if the confession were skillful enough . . . Maybe if it were set up right, with a suitable preface about the grimness of his experience, a first chapter devoted to his hatred of the burden, and a second designed to elicit her sympathy for what it cost him even to think of reopening the subject . . . Maybe it was just possible to wheedle—no, that would be a recognizably false note—to maneuver her into a position where she would have to see the temptation not to forgive as a potentially greater crime than anything he could possibly confess . . .

But that hope died too. There was no such fall-back position; the act would have to be performed without a net. He would make it across the wire or he would go down. She would either forgive him or she would not. So he tried for a while to believe that she would, and he thought of her goodness, her braveness and her openness . . . But then he thought of what he would actually have to confess to her: not only an inglorious past and a dismal present, but a future that would only be more of the same—and the attempt to believe simply collapsed at the feet of his certainty that no one could forgive that much.

And so it was that he came at last to what he had to do. There was a fourth option, but it was so unlike an option that he had not been able even to think of it until he had proved to himself that all the other doors were locked. It was the option of a corpse at its own funeral: lie there and get on with it. Forget the mock heroics of confessing and dying, the stagy *contrapposti* designed to convey the truth while wringing tears from the audience. There would be tears—Catharine had cried—but not at the poignancy of his repentance or the agony of his death, only at the sadness of having to deal for the last time with a life that had been dead for years. His confession was simply part of the obsequies; it was in order to nothing but a quick and decent burial. He could keep, if he liked, the hope of a resurrection, but only for what it was: no hope at all—just the mindless, inextinguishable flickering of the poker player's perpetual hunch that maybe, even on this last of all hands, by going shy on every bet . . .

*     *     *

He spent the rest of the morning at distractions in his office. He did not think of what he would say to her; time enough for that at noon. Instead, he formulated early in the day some general principles to govern the saying of it and he repeated them to himself like a litany. One: no names. Two: otherwise, tell it all: flat-out involvement where it was that, trifling where it was trifling, and with the numbers as accurate as possible. Three: don't explain, don't criticize, just state. Four: don't plead, don't manipulate, don't contrive, and don't hope. For once, admit you're dead, because for once you finally are.

When he drove over to the restaurant, he was quiet. He knew he would do it, and that was that.

9

Paul was five minutes early; Laura was five minutes late.

Waiting, he felt oppressed by the crass normality of his surroundings: the blacktop, the cars, the foundation planting of junipers, the brown-stained cedar shakes of the restaurant walls, the waterwheel turned by a trickle from an ill-concealed, three-quarter-inch pipe. Like the crowd at a wake, they were there on their own terms, not the corpse's—standing out in the sunlight swapping gossip and jokes, magnifying the enormity of death by paying no attention to it at all.

When she drove in, he walked over to her car.

"Listen. Before we have lunch, I want to talk to you about something. Do you have a minute?"

His bluntness and the foolishness of the question bothered him, but she took no apparent notice.

"Of course."

"Why don't you drive over to the far side of the lot and park there? It's quieter."

"All right."

She waited a few seconds.

"Don't you want to get in?"

"Oh. Sure."

He walked around and slid into the front seat. After

she parked, she turned off the ignition, rummaged in her purse for cigarettes, and put them on the hump in front of the gearshift. He asked if she needed a light.

"No. Talk first."

He looked at her once, exhaled, and fixed his eyes on the glove compartment latch.

"Look. I've never done this before, so I have no idea whether there's a better way to do it or not. Just let me run it out. First of all, I love you. That's true, and there's no way I could take it back even if I had to. But I have to tell you something. It's . . ."

He started to say, "It's probably not what you're afraid of," but that sounded like second guessing or manipulation and he broke off. Damn! He had hardly begun and it was beginning to go badly. He could feel in his bones the old Indian-wrestling skill itching for a chance to get into action, to set her off balance with a feint at Calling The Whole Thing Off—to play on her fear of being ditched—and then reassure her before getting around to what he really had to say. Resignedly, he began again.

"All right. I'll say it as straight as I can. No commentary, no embroidery. I got to where I'm at by thinking of being naked with you and wanting that more than anything in the world. That's not embroidery; at least I don't think it is. But anyway, the closer I got to the actuality, the more I realized I couldn't be naked with you—with *you*, not with just anybody—I couldn't be naked with you physically until I was mentally naked first. That's odd for me, because I've spent most of a lifetime covering up with people, keeping them in separate compartments, giving each one only as much information about me as I saw fit. I'm a hider, and my hiding has always been my armor.

Nobody ever got the whole story about me, except once. Even now, it'd probably be better left hidden. But I just can't leave it that way with you."

A long, explanatory parenthesis began to form itself in his mind: some background first, perhaps; then an account of the struggle over whether to tell her the truth and the discarding, one by one, of the three options; then finally an exposition of the deadness he felt. He threw it all away.

"Okay. No minced words. One way or another, I've been involved in a number of affairs. For years. And not only have I been, I am now. Not that I considered—or consider—them all love affairs. There was really only one I ever did. But that makes very little difference. I mean, it's no excuse, because whatever I may have had in mind, the women concerned thought they were love affairs, and I didn't do anything to disabuse them of the notion. Well, maybe all of them didn't think so. There were a couple who seemed to take it as just friendly sex, but most of them took it as romance with a capital "R." Which is why my mental reservation about having only one real love was nothing but a first-class gyp. It just meant that I was handing them a lot of attenuated devotion and allowing them to pick it up as if it were the deluxe article. Except in that one case. Being as honest as I can be, I still think I really meant that to be unqualified, even though all the messing around seems to argue against it. At least it was unqualified enough for me to confess to her what I'm telling you."

Obviously, there was an opening there for something. What? The results of that confession? No. That smelled like a self-serving comparison—a subtle challenge to Laura to do better when her turn came. Leave it.

"Look. This may be crass, but I promised myself I'd give you numbers. All told, over the years, maybe ten. Right now, four and a half: three flat-out and three not quite, with the not quites counted as halves. It's clear enough, isn't it? I mean that I'm confessing not just the past, but also the present and, as far as I can see, the future too? But I'm not asking for permission. I'm really not. It's inconceivable to me to ask for it. I know it sounds stupid, but I really would like to get out from under it all. It's just that, knowing what I know about myself, I can't see it happening. I want to end it, but I know I won't. It's a mess."

Laura had been watching him. She turned her head slightly and looked out through the windshield.

"The one . . . is she part of the four and a half?"

He took several seconds to pick up her meaning.

"No. That's all over. Washed up. A year ago."

She said nothing. In the silence he tried to think of what should come next. He felt as if there should now be some spate of words to breathe life into the dry bones he had scattered—some richer, more telling, more damning or excusing peroration to flesh them out; but he couldn't think of it. Suddenly, nakedly, he had come to the end. He had done, he supposed, what he set out to do: the corpse had been displayed. But it had been such an inadequate performance, such a perfunctory, mumbled funeral, such a tiny handful of dirt to throw on something so many years in the doing and so many hours in the repenting. But still it had been done, and with a certain miserable consistency at that: he had slopped through his life all the way, up to and including the end. If he had omitted details, he had at least conveyed the texture of it: it was a mess. Let it lie. He settled for a last, summary stab at clarity.

"There's not much more to say. I don't know if I'm really confessing guilt at sliding between all those sheets or not. I've had too many minds on that. For a couple of years there, I thought it was all right, and maybe I still do. All I know is that now that I want to give myself to you— God! it all sounds so corny and half-assed—now I want it to be different, but I just don't see any way out. I tell myself that the reason for that—for the inescapability, I mean, for not knocking it all off—is really kindness. You know: I've done enough damage by promising, the least I can do is suffer the consequences of my promises and hang in. But I don't know if that's a lie, or the truth, or half and half. To be honest, I probably think it's half and half. Which is just one more unacceptable idiocy. Let me shut up. All I know is that I love you and that I had to confess—to you, nobody else—the duplicity. That's the only point. So, Amen. Christ!"

For the first time, he turned and looked at her. The sun was in her hair and on her skin: rufous, warm. His resolve not to plead trembled for a second and then collapsed.

"One more thing. I wasn't going to say this, but it's at least as honest as the rest, so I will. When I look at you right now, I have the feeling that I'm separated by only the thinnest veil from someplace where everything is all right again—where I'm alive and not a mess anymore. But the veil is transparent steel or something and there's no way I can get past it. It might as well be a stone wall. In fact, it would be better if it were, because then I couldn't see the other side and long for it.

[ 68 ]

"It's like one of those drawings of a pile of blocks your eye normally reads one way, but if you can master the trick of looking at it, you can see the blocks reversed, flipped into another configuration. Looking at you, I want more than anything in the world for there to be another configuration; and somewhere, deep down, I think that maybe there might be. But I can't remember the trick of looking, and I'm left only . . ."

His next words would have been ". . . with this horrible sadness . . . ," but he never got them out.

"Paul?"

He stopped and was quiet. She reached over and touched his hand.

"You don't need to remember any trick."

"What do you mean?"

"You didn't have to tell me all that."

"Yes I did. At least, *I* did. I'm sorry you had to hear it, but I had to say it. No more fast shuffles. Not with you."

"I understand that. All I meant was I didn't have to be told. I knew."

"You knew?"

"Well, not the specifics. But I did know. It's just you, you know; just who you are. Maybe someday you'll have a choice about it; I don't know. All I know is, I have no choice. Last Monday, when you held me and kissed me in the back foyer over there, I was afraid of it—afraid that I wouldn't be able to take it, that I'd be hurt and go back on you. But then that was the end of it. I love you. There's no way of sorting it out."

He put his arms around her and buried his face in her neck. After a while he sat up and rubbed his eyes.

"You're incredible."

"I have clay feet too."

He let it pass.

"God! Do you realize what it's like to be able to stop trying to make yourself matter?"

She leaned over and kissed him.

"We matter. That's all. Take me to bed."

*       *       *

And that, finally, was that.

However, since Paul had not entertained even the possibility, it took him a minute to catch up with the fact.

"You mean, now?"

"Of course."

"No lunch?"

"No lunch."

"But where?"

"I don't know. Not in bucket seats. You decide."

"There's a motel a couple of miles past the shopping plaza. Is that all right?"

"Of course."

He sat back in the seat with a dazed smile on his face. For the first time, there was no more need to pretend.

"It'd be better if we used one car. Drive over to mine and we'll switch. Desk clerks never ask questions, but there's no sense providing the rest of the world with more evidence than it needs."

"Of course. I love you."

# 10

If this were a novel, it would be high time for something catalytic, if not cataclysmic, to obtrude itself upon Paul and Laura. They are almost, but not quite, bedded. Some disruptive or malevolent presence should now begin to hang over the proceedings; the roll in the hay that threatens so shamelessly and so effortlessly to happen should have at least a little body English put on it. A brush with discovery perhaps, or a pregnancy, or, failing all else, some mindless, external evil which the reader sees but the lovers know nothing of: a thirty-foot white shark, say, cruising the waters while they skinny-dip in a moonlit cove.

Unfortunately, however, I can give you nothing of the sort. I precluded discovery from the start; Laura's menstrual cycle is not propitious for conception; it is noontime; and I have just put them three miles from the nearest salt water. My one concession to novelistic development—the single obtrusive event in the history of their romance—has already occurred: it was the bumping of the shopping cart into the back of Paul's car. Admittedly that was hardly galvanic, let alone catalytic, but it is all you are going to get.

And the reason for that is that this is not a novel. It is a parable. The protagonist of a novel can be subjected to as many crosses and contretemps as credulity will put up with, but the main character of a parable can be allowed no problems at all. "Ah, but," you say. "What about the soul-searching of the prodigal son as he slopped hogs and sat among the husks? What about the painful screwing of his courage to the point of repentance and return? What, for that matter, about Paul's miserable morning just past?"

To which my answer is that you miss my point about the main character. But then, if it is any comfort to you, setting you up to miss the point of parables is practically the point of speaking in parables. They are told, after all, that seeing you might not see and hearing you might not understand. The major ones, in fact, are dimwittedly misnamed: they are not at all about what the popular imagination takes them to be about. The Laborers in the Vineyard, for example, is about the owner, not the laborers; the Prodigal Son is not about the prodigal, but the father.

Moreover, in the case of the latter—which is the germane one here—the popular imagination misses not one star performer, but two. In its genius for preferring the peripheral to the central, it ranks the prodigal as the major figure in the story and gives the elder brother second billing. In fact, however, the prodigal and his sour sibling are minor players; the star billing is reserved for two others: the father and the fatted calf. It pleases me that, in my version, Laura plays both parts.

To make her pregnant, therefore, or to toy with the prospect of feeding her to the fishes, would be as idle as having the father break a leg running down the path—as foolish as wondering whether it might not be a nice touch to have the servants rush back and report the fatted calf stolen. A little nail-biting and character development is allowable in a plausible, secondary character like Paul, but the implausible principal of the story—the divine surrogate whose role is to think the unthinkable and do the undoable—must sail through her accomplishment with not so much as a tangled sheet.

For at their heart, the parables are about a mystery of grace that makes mincemeat out of plausibility. The lesser lights in them may be made as fallible and accident-prone as you like because, after all, they are simply surrogates for us. Like us, they come through hardship to the stars. But the stars themselves—lights of the first magnitude like Laura—must be securely at home in mystery from the beginning. It is their role to reveal the blinding, mind-boggling news that God has no problems with sin. To give them problems, then—to hide their light under a bushel of trouble—is simply fatuous.

Accordingly, Laura's performance as the father, so flawless to this point, will continue to be so. And so will her tour de force in the role of the fatted calf. I said a minute ago that it was a co-starring role. But it is more. In some ways, it is the lead. The fatted calf is what the father's forgiveness is in order to. He wants his son home, not so they can spend their days in the confessional box, but so that, having gotten past that tiresome preliminary, they can both get on with the lavish party which is the specialty of their many-mansioned house—and of which the fatted calf is the supreme sacrament. Grace is in order to the celebration of life: "Let us eat and be merry, for this my son was dead, and is alive again; he was lost, and is found." Indeed, grace *is* the celebration of life, relentlessly hounding all the noncelebrants in the world. It is a floating, cosmic bash shouting its way through the streets of the universe, flinging the sweetness of its cassations to every window, pounding at every door in a hilarity beyond all liking and happening, until the prodigals come out at last and dance and the elder brothers finally take their fingers out of their ears.

It would have been better, therefore, if I had not provided Laura with a Volvo. Ideally, their celebrative congress should have occurred at the very moment of grace; the music and dancing should have burst immediately upon the scene in the instant when, with a smile, *La Exigenta* turned out to be a pussycat. Then and there on the spacious back deck of a nine-passenger wagon—preferably with fireworks in the grand tradition of Cary Grant and Grace Kelly—Paul should have availed himself of what, but for his estranged face, had been available to him from the start.

But it was a Volvo and Laura was right to sense, in bucket seats and floor-mounted shift, impediments to proper celebration. After all, even in the original parable it must have taken a while to get the stalled ox going properly. Her intuition that the best should never be served half-baked was simply one more perfection of her role. I urge you therefore to be patient. Their feast will not be as long in the preparing as the first one was.

But in the minutes it takes them to drive to their bed of green, or plaid, or whatever it will be, you and I should probably have a brief talk. I detect an ever so slight narrowing of your mind's eye, a small but potentially devastating question forming at the base of your brain—an incipient misunderstanding of what I am up to, which, if left uncorrected, could drive us light years apart.

You think, perhaps, that I am about to move too quickly from confession to celebration. "After all," you say, "Paul's honesty with Laura, commendable as it is, is hardly more than the first course of cinderblocks in the house of his eventual truthfulness. Might we not better wait awhile—at least, say, till the raising of the roof beam? Would it not be better to hold off the rewarding case of beer until he has leveled with, if not all concerned (we understand that telling his wife might be a bit tacky), then at least with the other four and a half, or six, or however many it really is, whom he has, by his own admission, been conning?"

Well. You raise a number of issues. Let me deal with them one by one.

First of all, your question betrays a misunderstanding of the nature of confession. It assumes that a confession, if the penitent is properly sincere, will not only make a difference in his life, but will make a difference for the good—that it is a kind of transaction in which a sufficiently humble, or painful, or embarrassing act of acknowledgment is automatically rewarded by a general distribution of the wherewithal for restoration and reform—that, in short, confession is good for the soul. But that, at best, is a very tricky half-truth. It must always be accompanied by a qualifier, namely: *but it all depends on whom you're dealing with.*

In the popular view, confession is thought of as a process of fixing up your own insides—of coming to yourself, as the prodigal did, and deciding finally to straighten up and fly right. But in truth, anyone who honestly comes to himself comes, not to the formulation of a new flight plan, but to the recognition that his life has the glide angle of a coke bottle and a broken one at that. True repentance leads only to the conclusion that the time for the repair of one's life is over and gone, and that one is in need not of a physician but of an embalmer—or, impossibly and unthinkably, *of someone who can raise the dead.*

The point is crucial. Confession is not the first step on

the road to recovery, it is the last step in the displaying of a corpse. And for that reason it can have only two natural effects on those before whom it is made: with luck, sadness; with none, disgust. But in any case, no one in his right mind will hang around very long. The cardinal rule of life is to have as little truck as possible with death. Accordingly, it is simply pointless to confess to anybody unless you are either prepared to stay dead or sure that the person you are dealing with is committed to, and capable of, raising the dead. Anyone up to less than that will just insist, glumly or gladly, on shoveling dirt onto your coffin.

Therefore, since no one ever knows for sure and in advance whether his confessor can really raise corpses (as Martha said when Jesus commanded the stone to be taken away from Lazarus' tomb: Resurrection is a neat idea, but what are the odds of its working with someone *this* dead?); and since in this vale of bookkeepers the chances of finding such a wonder-worker are slim indeed, the likeliest outcome of your scheme to have Paul let it all hang out in front of everybody will only be to provide him with six more pallbearers.

Which brings me to my second point. Your question belies a further confusion about the relationship between confession and reform. You seem to think that they are somehow causally intertwined, that confession will by its very nature initiate reform, and conversely that any confession not followed by reform is no true confession at all. But that is simply false. Confession is the admission of death; and death, obviously, is no position to cause anything—certainly not the conversion of its own deadness into a program of rehabilitation.

As a matter of fact, words like "reform" and "rehabilitation" should be ruled out of order. The only proper word here is *resurrection*. Confession is not a medicine leading to recovery. If we could recover—if we could say that beginning tomorrow or the week after next we would be well again—why then, all we would need to do would be apologize, not confess. We could simply say that we were sorry about the recent unpleasantness, but that, thank God and the resilience of our better instincts, it is all over now. And we could confidently expect that no one except a real nasty would say us nay.

But we never recover. We die. And if we live again, it is not because the old parts of our life are jiggled back into line, but because, without waiting for realignment, some wholly other life takes up residence in our death. Grace does not do things tit-for-tat; it acts finally and fully from the start. Laura moves into Paul irrevocably and without condition; the tide of her rises in the wreckage of his existence and becomes his life. Not a supplement to it, not a corrective of it. Just *it,* just *everything.* In one instant, by his faith in her grace, he becomes what Luther called the saved man: *simul justus et peccator,* a just man and a sinner at the same time. Just, because she accepts him; and a sinner still, because in her love she will not wait to do it.

Shockingly, then, it will be no skin off Paul's nose if he is still screwing around; it will be skin off Laura's. It will be nails through her hands and feet, thorns on her head, a spear wound in her side. He is saved by the impetuosity of her love, and he is saved far too soon. But he is saved.

And that is terrible. And when you see the awfulness of it—when you finally understand the cost at which you have been loved into life . . . well, there is reason *there* for

for reform, if you want to use the word. But the reform will be like nothing you once expected. It will be mostly tears and sorrow. Not a going from strength to strength, but a lifetime of penance in the presence of the sacred, wounded head, a perpetual standing beneath the cross to mourn the well-beloved, yet thank her for her death.

Grace uses no sticks and no carrots. It just dies for our life. That is no doubt more unfair to all concerned than any tit-for-tat arrangement the world would ever make, but it is the only way we can live. If we saw it clearly, we would cry our eyes out over the sadness of it. But that is how it is: our joy comes by another's blood and from wounds we open all our lives.

Once again, then, don't be in a hurry to shove people into confessing to everybody on the block. It's hard enough to find someone willing to forgive; it's even harder to accept it when you do. It is quite sufficient for Paul to confess to Laura alone.

*     *     *

Besides. Parables are told only because they are true, not because the actions of the characters in them can be recommended for imitation. Good Samaritans are regularly sued. Fathers who give parties for wayward sons are rightly rebuked. Employers who pay equal wages for unequal work have labor troubles. And any shepherd who makes a practice of leaving ninety-nine sheep to chase after a lost one quickly goes out of the sheep-ranching business.

The parables are true because they are like what God is like, not because they are models for us to copy. It is simply a fact that the one thing we dare not, under any circumstances, imitate is the only thing that can save us.

The parables are, one and all, about the foolishness by which grace raises the dead. They apply to no sensible process at all, only to the divine insanity that brings everything out of nothing.

# 11

Their bed, as it turned out, was indeed green. At least the bedspread was. And since it took an hour for them to get around to removing it, green was the background of their love. That, and silence.

After they were inside, he turned the privacy lock, tested it, and took her in his arms. His hands, at first joined behind the small of her back, parted and circled her waist. The muscles below her diaphragm contracted at the touch of his fingers. Her left leg moved forward and outward a little against his right. His first physical impression of her—his surprise at her chasteness—had been wrong. It wasn't chasteness, it was subtlety. She just began at a whisper.

He dropped his hands from her waist to her rump and, spreading his fingers as wide as he could, cupped them over the astonishing fullness of her. There was an answering contraction once again. He smiled a great, boyish grin and held her hard. Her wrists lay on his shoulders, her fingers at the nape of his neck. She half lowered, half turned her head and made a gesture of looking under her arm to where his hands were resting. Then she beamed back at him with the look of a child who has startled someone by jumping out of hiding.

There are people who are in touch with their bodies and there are people who are not. But even among those who are, there is a further distinction to be made. Women of exquisite proportions are so used to inspiring reverence that they begin eventually to take themselves with a gravity that befits the keeper of the shrine. But women with features of exceptional generosity carry in themselves a mirth waiting only for some questing heart's astonishment to set it free. To make love to such a woman is to be let in on a lurking hilarity, to discover at the moment of one's own surprise at her pendulousness or her depth—or, in the instant case, at the grandeur of Laura's Seat—a corresponding hidden laughter in her, a delicious self-satisfaction by which she answers her lover's amazement with a knowing and gleeful "Of course." Far from inviting piety, great breasts or buttocks call forth the coarse denominations of the eighth-grade vocabulary—or, in the case of the learned, they make irreverent puns race through the mind: *Sedia sapientiae; What is the chief end of man?*

But that is for old lovers. New ones just laugh in awkward delight and move on. Without letting go of the basis of their private joke, Paul backed her to the bed and fell on her.

Harold Ross, the first editor of the *New Yorker,* always insisted quite seriously that nothing was indescribable. There are some things, however, that are not worth describing seriously and chief among them has to be the unrehearsed and unrehearsable ritual by which two people undress each other for the first time. Its only saving grace is that it is done *obiter* to something worth a trip through a minefield of vexations.

It begins with deceptive ease at the unbuttoning of blouse and shirt, respectively. But then. Arms do not come out of sleeves easily when bodies are lying down.

The lovers disengage, therefore, and sit up. His shirt comes off with some dispatch; her blouse collar enmeshes itself in her necklace and their progress comes to a grinding halt. For the first of several times in the rite, the sacred words, "Here, let me" are uttered while she unclasps the offending jewelry.

Next, of course, the bra. For all our supposed liberation from inhibitions to sexual freedom is it not odd that the twentieth century has made but a single contribution to the female wardrobe that can be conveniently removed? I have in mind the half-slip. But what good is that? To have thus liberated the upper half of the female body only to render it inaccessible by a brassiere hook of a design unimproved since the time of Boss Tweed . . . Why, it is easier for a camel to pass through the eye of a needle—no, more aptly, it is easier for a woman to tie a boy's tie from behind than for a man to undo a woman's bra from the front. The only solution again is, "Here, let me."

By this time, however, the point of the exercise threatens to recede to an infinite distance, so they make such love as is possible in their intermediate state until the *terminus ad quem* begins to heave into sight once more. But then they have no choice but to resume, all thumbs, the interrupted interruption. Her skirt must be addressed: zipper and button must be found and conquered. Next, his pants: first the belt buckle; then a pause while, one-handedly, she worries the hook fastener in vain. Finally, "Here, let me."

In the end, however, they reach an end. But by such means! After five thousand years of recorded civilization and twenty Christian centuries, the ultimate step in undressing a contemporary woman is a gesture worthy only of a caveman: skirt, half-slip, pantyhose, and pants are seized as if they had one common waistband and hauled off in a single motion. The motion is such, however, that while it achieves the immediate end, it places the achiever approximately six paces from the end ultimately desired—and standing on his feet at that.

While he is up, therefore, he sits himself down on the corner of the bed, unlaces his shoes, removes his pants and, in frustration at what can only be a conspiracy on the part of the universe to kill enthusiasm with the boredom of routine, stops short at that and makes love with his socks on.

*     *     *

Laura gasped a little as he entered her, then took him home. As far as he could tell from the soft, high whimper, she came immediately.

The exaltation of simultaneous orgasm as the Best Of All Possible Ways to Make Love is another obfuscation foisted on us by the modern world. There are times and places, of course, when it is a nice, surprising touch, an interesting minor variation in the enjoyment of a great and complex good. But to insist that two people cannot truly do justice to the feast of feasts unless they proceed through it in contrived equality—she not finishing the last grape on her *Sole Veronique* until he has eaten his; he not consuming a single *pomme soufflé* except in perfect synchrony with her; and both holding off the enjoyment of the ultimate spoonful of *fraises au crême fraiche* until they can take it together and say, Ahhh!—why, it reduces the feast to an Alphonse and Gaston routine. It is fun if it just happens, but only people who are a little funny ever try deliberately to bring it off.

Laura, therefore, was through her first course before Paul had done much more than touch his wine. But, sane man that he was, he was pleased at her pleasure and without asking fetched seconds.

They lay still. He kissed her eyes, her face, her mouth, then lifted himself a little on his elbows.

"Hey, are you safe? I mean there's no point in getting you pregnant is there."

"It's all right. It's just after my period."

"You mean you're not on anything? No pill? No loop?"

"Nope. Just rhythm. I'm absolutely regular. It's perfectly all right."

"Not in my book. Too many variables, all of which you discover only after the first variation. All you need is to ovulate three days too early after making love to somebody with one sperm cell that lives three days too long. The odds are against it, of course. But don't forget, the house always has the odds figured in its own favor, and you and I aren't exactly part of the establishment here. This is Vatican roulette, and the world is full of losers who thought they had a system."

"Well, I've never lost yet. So far as I'm concerned, it really is safe."

"Bosh! I think *I'll* hold back, just to be sure. Don't worry, though. The cloud has a silver lining. Men are too soon over; this way, I can make love to you all afternoon."

The entrée, when served, was apparently even better than the *poisson* and he lost count after her third helping, delighted only that the kitchen was able to keep up with her appetite. But in the hour it took before she finally rested, he also lost something more than count. He lost his lifelong preoccupation with counting—and with all the other self-conscious conjurings by which the shaky sexual ego tries to instill confidence in itself. For that one hour, he found himself at last and for the first time gladly beyond the whole subject of sex. He was sustained not by his own efforts, which heretofore were frequently in vain and often short-lived, but simply by her. She held him in her, she moved upon him, she surprised him with herself. And when he finally realized, after long love, how different it all was with her, he tried to tell her. But all she said was, "I love your body."

She kissed his chest and his neck, his eyes, his lips, and the cleft of his chin.

"How do you shave in there?"

It was a line from an old Cary Grant movie and it pleased him that she thought it up, apparently without knowing so.

"You just work at it—and you cut yourself a lot. Actually, it was only half as deep when I first started shaving, but over the years I've excavated it into a real archaeological dig."

She held herself close to him. He ran his hands through her hair, his palms close to her head, the chestnut fullness of it gripped in the roots of his fingers. Finally he spoke.

"You please me, Love."

Some words hit like cold water. The easy, neutral endearment "Love" reminded him with a shock of who and where he was. Like the philanderer in the Italian movie who called all his mistresses "Tesora," Paul had made a point of seldom using any woman's proper name for fear of crossing wires. But here he was now, using the old, cagey generality in the arms of the new and saving particular—a sinner in the very thick of his justification. He was not past his deadness, as he first imagined; he still carried the moribund collection of former lives within him.

What to do, then? Rinse out the offending mouth by working the name "Laura" into the conversation a certain number of times over the next five minutes as a kind of penance? He decided not. Let it pass, at least for now. Eventual congruence with the new order was inevitable, of course; but faking out a present congruence was just earning brownie points for yourself. And cheap, misleading ones at that. She had said, "It's just you; just who you are." If she didn't have to sort, neither did he. His fidelity, at last, was no longer to himself.

They were quiet for a long time. Paul stroked her hair and said, "What are you thinking?"

"I was thinking how I like it when you say, 'You please me.'"

"You really do, Love. Oh God, you really do."

\*         \*         \*

Eventually they separated and lay side by side on the bed. She pulled up the edge of the bedspread and tried to cover herself.

"You cold?"

"A little."

"Here, sit up."

With a series of trampoline bounces, they pulled off the spread, turned down the top covers, and slid in. He pulled the blanket up and tucked it around her neck.

"Better?"

"Much."

"Too bad I didn't bring some wine. But then, that

wasn't really a possibility, was it? Anyway, I'm not *very* sorry."

A joke ran through his mind, a mock statistic about American men: after intercourse, fifteen percent light up a cigarette, ten percent reach for a drink, and seventy-five percent get up and go home. He didn't tell it. Why? Too offhand? Too cynical, too close to home for her sensibilities? No. The reason was not in her but in himself. This time he caught the old man before he threw out the line, or better said, caught the old hider before he pulled his famous disappearing act and jumped behind a joke to avoid the consequences of closeness. Instead, he put his arm around her and drew her to him. She lay her head on his shoulder and spoke against his chest.

"You know? All my life, I've known I would be here . . . Well, maybe not all. Maybe just since I was seven or eight . . ."

"How do you mean?"

"I don't know. I just always knew that I was never at home anywhere, but that I would be someday . . . and this is it."

What occurred to him to say sounded extravagant, but he said it anyway. No man, having put his hand to the plow, and looking back . . .

"That's good. Because you are. You're my love. I'm yours."

She repeated the words slowly.

"I'm your love. And you are mine."

She lifted herself suddenly on one elbow and went on rapidly.

"I know this sounds funny, but for a long time I just couldn't believe that I was a body. I don't mean not anybody. I mean not a body at all. And that's weird, because

I really am in touch with my own body—I sense when anything is out of line. I'm almost never sick, but when I am, I hate it. And when it's not just one thing that's out of line, but sort of everything—when it's not just being ill, but a kind of not being there at all . . .

She faltered. He waited for her, saying nothing.

"When it's like that, it's like being dead. But that's over now. You're my life."

He kissed her again.

"That's hard to believe. As far as I'm concerned, it's the other way around. And when it comes to your thinking you're not a body. God! You are the most bodily woman I've ever known. Every move says so. It's just inconceivable to me that you could sense yourself the way you obviously do and still not know that."

"That's only sense. It works two ways. If you can't believe in your own being, it makes you feel worse—like going through the motions with no hope. It makes you feel like a mourner at your own funeral."

"I know."

"Good, she said, then slid herself to a sitting position against the headboard and lit a cigarette. She held his head with her right hand and smoked in silence for awhile.

"You know why I think you give me back my body? I read somewhere that in the order of nature, places create persons, but that in the order of grace, persons create place. I'm not sure what that means, but it seems to fit. Before you, everything felt as if it was nowhere, so I was nothing too. But with you . . . we create a place . . ."

"And the place then proceeds to create us. Right? Nature, to grace, and back to nature."

"Yes. That's really true, you know. The last step is to

discover what you were from the beginning."

He waited till she finished her cigarette.

"What time do you have?"

"I don't want to look."

"You're being a brat. By your own admission."

"That's right."

"All I want to do is be sure we don't get ourselves in the position of having to tear unceremoniously out of here. There should be a leisure about it. But since we do have to leave eventually . . ."

"I don't want to leave. Why should we?"

"You're right. There are a dozen reasons why, and there's no reason. But we will. So what time is it?"

"Two twenty-five."

"Perfect. I don't have to be back till four. Come. Take a shower with me."

She slid down and kissed him.

"That's better. I love you."

# 12

Paul adjusted the water temperature, pulled up the bypass on the spigot and, when the shower was running properly, spread a towel on the bottom of the tub.

"Safety first. Who needs a broken hip to explain?"

She smiled and said, "You're marvelous," as if she were admiring some vast wisdom. She seemed to take only pleasure in his obvious savoir-faire, perfectly aware of the circumstances of its acquisition, yet somehow unbothered by the awareness. One can imagine the father of the returned prodigal with such a smile. The elder brother, perhaps, has turned up with yet another of the overripe tomatoes he insists on picking for girlfriends, and the father, sitting on the veranda with his younger son, shakes his head in silent sadness as he watches the couple leave. After they are out of earshot the prodigal shakes his head too and says, "Christ! All she's got is a wiggle: her brains must have fallen into her ass." And the father smiles and thinks to himself, "At last! Who cares where he learned it? Finally I've got somebody who knows what the score is."

They stood in the shower and soaped each other. Once again, the ritual is not indescribable, but it is slightly overrated. What is memorable about it is not the operation itself. That is simply a mixture of routine and fuss: it takes time to lather two bodies, the soap drops at least once and their freedom of motion is strictly limited by the necessity of keeping her hair dry. What stays in the mind is only the smoothness with which two bodies slide upon each other, the sense of liberation from the drag of friction. That, and the chasteness of the rinsing.

They got out and dried each other, but when they opened the door into the room the blast of cold air set her shivering hard and he took her back under the covers. She lay in his arms till the chattering stopped, then sat up a little with the blanket pulled around her.

"It's a voluntary crucifixion, you know."

The phrase came at him out of nowhere and made him distinctly uneasy. But he was learning fast to wait her out and he did. She had a knack for misleading opening lines.

"I know I'm a brat about leaving you, but that's exactly what I ought to be. Men and women are different, I think. Men don't think about being separated from someone they love until the minute it has to happen. I guess they feel it just as much after that, but a woman feels it all the time, even when she's making love. She carries the pain of separation inside her, always feeling it, but just deliberately ignoring it. That's why I react the way I do when you ask me what time it is. For you, knowing the time is a way of figuring how much longer you've got before the pain starts; for me, it's just a recognition of the pain that's already there, and the beginning of the wait until it kills me."

"I never thought of it that way. Too bad there's always sadness."

"But that's all right. The sadness is inside the joy. At least it is as long as you keep it there—as long as you keep telling it it's not allowed to be the main thing. That's why it's a *voluntary* crucifixion. And it's all right to complain about it. Jesus was a brat in Gethsemane."

God! he thought. You really did have to wait her out. Jesus, of all things! And at a time like this! He had expected her opener about crucifixion to be a lead to some second thoughts about his unreliability, but he had heard only the word "crucifixion," not the word "voluntary." If he had said anything he would have missed her point by a mile: she wasn't afraid of pain, at least not once she willed it. And apparently the only pain she was having trouble willing was not the pain of possible hurt from him—that she really had accepted for good in the back foyer of the restaurant—it was simply the pain of separation.

Which reminded him of something.

"You know that passage from the *Horae Canonicae* I said I'd memorize for you? Well, I did; but there was something in it I'd forgotten about, and it bothered me when I came across it. The whole poem is about Good Friday, but the verse I was quoting had the words, 'what happened to us from noon till three.' I don't know, I guess it was just that that was the time we spent at lunch on Monday and I didn't want to bring up anything that mentioned the possibility of pain coming out of it. And today it just never came up till you said 'separation'—that's in it too—and suddenly it all fell together: Monday and today, from noon till three. Crucifixion. Separation. Weird."

"Not really. It's another validation. Anyway, I looked the poem up myself while you were gone. That's probably why crucifixion came into my head. Recite it for me."

He sat up and tilted back his head.

Nothing is with me now but a sound,
A heart's rhythm, a sense of stars

Leisurely walking around, and both
Talk a language of motion
I can measure but not read: maybe
My heart is confessing her part
In what happened to us from noon till three,
That constellations indeed
Sing of some hilarity beyond
All liking and happening,
But, knowing I neither know what they know
Nor what I ought to know, scorning
All vain fornications of fancy,
Now let me, blessing them both
For the sweetness of their cassations,
Accept our separations.

He made a small wave with his hand.

"Now that I hear it, the coincidences are more verbal than substantive. Still, they're coincidences."

"And therefore they still work—they still validate."

"You know something, Love? Your mind sails a course that comes within one degree of being just plain kooky, but I've never yet caught you crossing the line. Sometimes I think I have, but when I try to prove it, I end up agreeing with you. Of course, that could mean nothing more than that I'm over the line too. Who knows?"

"What did I say?"

"Oh, the business about the coincidences still validating. It sounds as if you're hell-bent to get validation and you'll take any liberties you need with the meaning in order to get them—like those Shakespeare nuts who find astrological cryptograms in the Sonnets. But then I think of some things I've said about the imagination—how the power of images isn't confined to the discursive framework, but operates all over the lot, sometimes parallel to it, sometimes not—and I say what the hell, Auden isn't talking about the same separation we're talking about, but separation is separation, and every example of it, once admitted by name to the mind, has full power of the image. So it perfectly well could be validation, and therefore you're still sane. Or at least you're no crazier than I am."

"Good. While you're being a compulsive pedant, what's a cassation?"

"A serenade. Actually it has two meanings, and the pun is intended. Cassation as *serenade* comes from the German *Gasse, street*—a street song; but it also has a French derivation, from *cour de cassation,* the final court of appeal. A cassation in that sense is a quashing, a settling, a cessation, an ending. So: the poem is called *Compline;* it's about the end of the day, about going to sleep, which is an image of death; but it's also about Good Friday, so this is sleep under the shadow of the crucifixion, another image of death; but then the cross is the image of reconciliation, too:

> Garlic and sapphires in the mud
>   Clot the bedded axle tree . . .
> Below, the boarhound and the boar
>   Pursue their pattern as before
> But reconciled among the stars

And there you have the constellations singing, the music of the spheres harmonized into hilarity again—and I've also gotten Eliot into the act for good measure, but it doesn't matter whether he or Auden came first because once the images are in the mind their powers are concurrent and the voltage just builds and builds till it starts arcing all over the place, validating any damn thing you please."

[ 94 ]

He pulled her down on the bed, rolled over on her, and kissed her.

"You win, Love. I give up."

"How come you're on top, then?"

"Because you put me there."

"I did?"

"Of course. Don't try to be logical. It doesn't become you."

They gathered up their clothes and dressed separately, she in the bathroom, he in the room itself. He put on everything except his shoes and socks, then sat in the armchair and lit his pipe. He thought again about having called her "Love." He didn't like it. But what do you do when all the words are used up? Call her something you can't believe yourself saying? Let it stand.

She came out of the bathroom combing her hair, dressed except for shoes.

"You got me wet."

"We got you wet. That's the biggest charge I'll plead to. Anything more and I call my lawyer."

"All right. We're both guilty. What do I sentence us to?"

He winced again. But at the end of the chute, just before you go into the millwheel, what do you say?

"Life."

She said nothing. Instead, she went back into the bathroom and fussed some more. Damn! Independent kookiness was one thing, but not to respond to a line like that! Eventually though, she called out to him.

"You know? I knew we'd be lovers. A year ago."

Hell! She had him by the short hair.

"How'd you know that?"

"At the end of the first course of yours I took . . .

There was this sort of sad girl who always seemed to be on the edge of everything—I think her name was Meredith or something dreamy like that, which just made her extra sad because it sounded so romantic, but all her romances were nothing but disasters—well, she asked me— I remember, it was the last day of the course—'Hey, are you and he lovers?' And I just said, 'No.' But I also thought, 'Someday though, if you ask me again, I'll have a chance to lie to you.' "

She came out of the bathroom and quietly, almost gravely, went and knelt in front of him. Sitting back on her heels, she looked at him, then bowed herself to the floor and kissed his feet.

He bent over to raise her.

"Hey. What's that for? I can't vouch for my feet."

She sat up.

"Your feet are clean enough. I'm yours."

He touched her face, her lips, her hair, in silence— and finally, *post longa exsilia,* he cried.

She took his head in her hands and kissed his eyes.

"Call me before six?"

"Sure. Can I see you Monday?"

"Yes. I'll figure something out before you call."

*     *     *

Nostrum est interim mentem erigere
et totis patriam votis appetere,
et ad Jerusalem a Babylonia
post longa regredi tandem exsilia.

# 13

It is a good place to leave them for a while—and it is the best of all possible last lines to leave them with. I apologize for the Latin, but it is a stanza from the hymn *O quanta qualia sunt illa sabbata* by Peter Abelard. The theme is heaven's endless sabbaths, and it was written by him for use at Saturday vespers in the Convent of the Paraclete—of which Heloise was abbess. So if you are upset with me for crossing sexual and theological wires, reconsider your position. Better men than I have done it before—at higher prices, and with greater effect. Apparently, they found it worth the effort. If you doubt my word, however, reread the last chapters of Rose Macauley's *The Towers of Trebizond.* It will make your hair stand on end.

In any case, though, it is a superb last line. I hate to give you the hymnal version of it, because it misses the joyous immediacy of the Latin. Still, as I write this, it is the feast day of blessed John Mason Neale, who translated it, so it's unthinkable not to give him equal space:

Now in the meanwhile, with hearts raised on high,
We for that country must yearn and must sigh,
Seeking Jerusalem, dear native land,
Through our long exile on Babylon's strand.

There, we're even.

\*　　　　\*　　　　\*

You notice, of course, that suddenly you and I seem to have no company but each other's. Paul and Laura have been suitably launched: the vessel of their romance has slid down the ways and out onto the face of the deep. If it did not happen without some friction and heat, it at least came off without untoward event—which was, if you will recall, all I promised you. So here we are, ready at last to make our own beginning at understanding it.

If I assess your mood correctly, you are still of two minds. On the one hand, you wish Paul and Laura well (as who would not?). You see clearly, in your heart of hearts, that the brave really do deserve the fair and vice-versa, and that there is no other way of bringing about the eschatological realization of that proposition—given the case histories of the brave and the going price of the fair—than by the foolishness of grace. You are glad, in short, as any sinner would be, that she did not stick at being stuck—that she was to Paul what the Gospel tells us God himself is to us all, the gracious and ultimate stuckee.

On the other hand, however, you carry in your head, at a respectful if not infinite distance from your heart of hearts, a Resident Moral Theologian who politely but firmly takes continual exception to your gladness. He suggests that surely something more than this parable of wishful folly is necessary if we are to plumb the depths of the mystery by which we are finally restored. He, in short, cannot stand the fact that before long Paul is probably going to climb into bed with one of his previous partners.

Let me review for you some of the devices by which your house moralist approaches this problem. He is not an unreasonable fellow, and he makes at least some effort to reach a compromise with your heart.

He first argues that the situation might be rendered acceptable if Paul undertook, successfully, to avoid any *new* promiscuities. He very nearly perfects a line of argument that holds that lapses into sexual congress with *former* colleagues between the sheets can be viewed as occurring under a kind of adjournment *sine die,* and accordingly may be, if not recommended, at least seen as included in the death to which Laura's grace triumphantly brings the power of resurrection.

But then he makes some typical moral theologian's errors. First of all, he begins to harp on the word "successfully" which he improvidently included in his reasoning. He forgets that from Laura's point of view her grace was antecedent to *all* the unsuccesses Paul laid before her and would, as long as it remained grace at all, have the same attitude toward subsequent lapses as it had to preceding ones. But second, he subtly insinuates into his thinking the idea of a *minimum condition* and lodges it in the very concept of grace, thus leading himself to postulate that, while Laura may reasonably be expected to put up with Paul's recidivism vis-à-vis Janet (to take the next to the most difficult case) or (in the most difficult case of all) with Catharine (this is a tremendous concession on his part, but he does understand the explosive power of the buried past, he does have a heart—located, unfortunately, in his head), he is not about to let grace write out a permission slip for Paul to sleep with some tramp in a motel in Monticello.

Having introduced this note of condition, however, he has effectively lost sight of grace and it is only a matter of time before he arrives back at law. Next, therefore, he includes a further condition: not only must Paul sleep scrupulously alone in Monticello; he must, on some reasonable timetable, begin to phase out Janet & Co. Congruence with grace (and note, please, what a contradiction in terms that is: congruence with the ultimate incongruity) becomes the condition *sine qua non* of its bestowal. And so he comes to his inevitable emendation of Romans 5:8, "But God commendeth his love toward us, in that, while we were yet sinners, Christ died for us, *on the condition that after a reasonable length of time we would be the kind of people no one would ever have had to die for in the first place. Otherwise, the whole deal is off.*"

The gentleman in your head, you see, is a menace. At least I consider him so in spite of his good intentions. Accordingly, there is nothing for it but for you and me to sit here and grapple in earnest with the classic text on this whole guilt-edged, blame-filled business, Romans 6:1 ff:

> What shall we say then? Shall we continue in sin, that grace may abound?
> God forbid. How shall we, that are dead to sin, live any longer therein?

# 14

Let me, once again, gloss the text for you.

*What shall we say then? Shall we continue in sin that grace may abound?*

*What shall we say then?* The Apostle begins with a question because he has raised a question. He has said flatly at the end of chapter five that sin cannot hold a candle to grace: "But where sin abounded, grace did much more abound." All Paul's liaisons, laid end to end, are not as wide as one hair of Laura's head.

But he sees clearly that in saying that he has opened a loophole to every immoral opportunist in the world. Worse yet, he has gotten himself in dutch with the moralists, all of whom are ready to scream "permissiveness!" at the drop of anything that even looks like an opportunity. Therefore he puts the opportunist's gleeful spotting of the loophole in the moralist's dour mouth and boldly asks the question at its worst.

*Shall we continue,* he asks (the Greek is ἐπιμένωμεν, shall we "stay on, abide still, continue in"). But continue, stay, abide in what? In a pursuit of life, liberty and happiness? In some course of action, in some possible series of choices? No. *In sin* (τῇ ἁμαρτίᾳ—not a verb, not an action word at all, but a noun, and in the dative case): in a state of sin; in a state that for Paul was the same thing as death; in that centerless, lifeless nowhere of his former being—in that still smashed terminus at which, after Catharine and before Laura, he had been deposited, seedy and by himself.

But consider this death of sin to which the Apostle refers: death does not rise; only life does. He does not ask this rhetorical question to tell Paul he *ought* not to continue in sin. He does it to tell him he *cannot*. And for a very simple reason: Paul is dead. He has no "I," no living ego, no effective, vivifying, interambient self with which to make the attempt. He is a corpse, not a body; parts, not a whole. *Shall we continue in sin?* is a foolish question, not because it proposes an inadvisable action, but because it proposes it to a totally nonexistent actor. There is no "we," no Paul, to do any continuing, whether in sin or in anything else. We have not lost our powers; we have lost our identity. Paul is not enfeebled; he is shot. There is, as he finally found when he tried to rouse himself to love Laura, simply nobody worth bothering to call Paul.

And therefore when he was raised to life again by her grace, when the tide of her flowed like living water into the dead wreckage of his being, it was not the old Paul that rose, but a new one—the work, not of Paul, but of that wholly other life whose name became his soul. His concupiscent former existence—no, I want it stronger than that—even his screwed-up present situation is no life at all. It remains death, and the Paul who brought it about remains dead for all eternity. Laura is the only life he has; his life is hid in her. "I live," he says; "yet not I, but Laura who lives in me." She is his resurrection. Her "We matter. That's all. Take me to bed" was nothing less than "Lazarus, come forth."

Small wonder then that the Apostle mocks his own question with *God forbid.* The question is not only rhetorical, it is ridiculous—a patent contradiction in terms. *Paul? Continue in sin?* Come now, he says. How can a nobody choose to continue in nothing? Talk sense, man, or don't talk at all. There is only one Paul now, and when he hears his own voice speaking at the center of his life, he hears: Laura, Laura, Laura. And there is only one continuance now that sends his roots rain and that, too, is Laura, Laura, Laura. As the Apostle might have said had he written more fully of his own experience: "For me, to live is Christ. I am dead and my life is hid with Christ in God. You ask me about someone named Saul. Let me think. Saul? Ah, yes. I remember a Saul I knew once. But that was in another country; and besides, the poor bastard is dead. Jesus, Jesus, Jesus."

You still do not see? You feel I am forcing the parable? Let me put it another way.

Do me the favor of focusing your mind very narrowly on the last scene between Paul and Laura. Get all the moral baggage out of the picture. And forget about whether the emotional fervor of that moment will, a week or a year hence, survive. I am trying to capture the force of what the Apostle is saying, not calculate the actuarial risk of writing a policy on it.

In that moment, therefore . . . in that moment only, when she knelt and kissed his feet and said "I am yours" . . . in that one instant of recognition, when at last after long exile he found himself alive in Jerusalem again . . . in that single burst of tears, when his captivity was finally over and the songs of Zion were on his tongue in no strange land . . . do you seriously think that then and there he hankered for some corner bar in Babylon—that, while Laura kissed his eyes, he had the least interest, say, in making out with Janet?

Of course you do not. And in your further wisdom you see that the possibility of his future declination from that height of awareness has nothing to do with the case. You see that such a "fall from grace" would not be a fall from grace at all. At the very most it would be a fall from faith, a piece of stupid mindlessness by which he ceased to apply himself to the only life he had.

But do you also see something else? Do you see that to lose faith is not to lose grace? That to return to death is a radically meaningless act, because we remain alive even in that return by the unlosable grace that insists on our resurrection willy-nilly? Do you see that Christ raises *all* the dead, the just and the unjust, the faithful and the faithless alike? And that he raises them *now?*

Suppose that in a week or a year Paul does revisit Babylon. Suppose he goes back to his death. Suppose even that he does it again and again. Ah! Now you see, perhaps, why I was so shirty about not giving Laura any hangups: as long as her grace remains grace, she remains the only life he has—even while he is whoring around in some Babylonian dive. Whether he behaves or misbehaves, he is dead from start to finish but for her. Unchanging, unswerving, she goes on being his resurrection, the one center at which his sins are always forgiven. All he has to do the seventh time or the seventy-times-seventh time is the same thing he did the first time: confess, admit once more the truth of his abiding death, and trust once again the life that never left him for a second.

Only an idiot, the Apostle says, could ever confuse that with permission. St. Paul is not talking about morality at all; morality is for the living. He is talking about death; and the only thing that makes sense when you have to deal with the dead is resurrection. He is not pointing out some possible course of action whose permissibility or impermissibility might be a matter of debate (you have, after all, always had permission, within wide limits, to go ahead and do any damn fool thing you wanted to); rather, he is pointing out a metaphysical impossibility: you can't get away from the love that will not let you go; when the Resurrection and the Life says "Lazarus, come forth," the rest of the story does not depend on Lazarus. He can drag his feet all the way—admittedly a Hell of a thing to do—but he rises, no matter what. He just plain does.

The Apostle, however, goes even further. Not content with setting up the permission-seeking opportunist and the opportunity-hating moralist as idiots, he presses his case and makes complete fools of them: *Shall we continue in sin,* he has them ask, *that grace may abound?*

Do you see? He is tricking them into an even more glaring metaphysical impossibility than the first. He is having them suggest that there is some way in which sin can stand in a *causal* relationship with grace, some way that death, on its own motion, can produce resurrection—that Laura's love, in short, can somehow be an effect of Paul's having bedded other women. But her grace, of course, is not an effect of anything Paul does, good or bad. It is, at its root, uncaused by anything outside herself at all. Grace makes itself abound. There is no way—and no need—of forcing its hand.

Which is why, then, the Apostle begins verse 2 with *God forbid* (μὴ γένοιτο). There is a problem of translation here. The "God forbid" of the King James Version catches the urgency of the Greek, but the word "God" simply isn't in the original: that just says something like "Let it not happen." Other versions render it in various ways. The Revised Standard Version says, "By no means," which catches St. Paul's meaning better, but sounds far too relaxed. And the Vulgate translates it, *Absit,* which means, literally, "Let it be absent."

I propose, therefore, that we cut our losses, capitalize on the distinctive merits of each of these several versions, and combine the result in one new rendering. Let us keep the urgent negativity of the King James Version's *God forbid!;* the almost Yiddish nuance of *It shouldn't happen!* in the original Greek; the refreshing note of *Get out of here with that jazz!* from the Latin *Absit;* and the sense of simple, literal impossibility in the Revised Standard Version's *By no means!*—meaning, there just isn't any way.

The locution that seems to me best suited to combine them all is the phrase *No way!* Accordingly, my version reads as follows:

> *Shall we continue in sin, that grace may abound?*
> *No way! How shall we, who are dead to sin, live any longer therein?*

Perhaps now you see; though if you do not, it is not entirely your fault. Not only is St. Paul's point difficult to grasp; its difficulty is compounded by the Apostle himself later on in the chapter when he nods a little and lets his own resident moral theologian sneak a couple of verbs in the imperative mood into verses 12 and 13 ("Let not sin therefore reign in your mortal bodies . . . neither yield ye your members as instruments of unrighteousness. . . .") He seems, for a moment, to slip back into mere commandment again, to be laying down the law in the old style; and since the human race can never hear law promulgated without wondering what the penalty is, we imagine the only penalty possible and conclude that the implied condition is: " . . . because if you don't behave, God will take his grace away from you." To be sure, St. Paul rouses himself at the end of the chapter and closes on the clear note of grace as a free and unqualified gift. But the damage is done, and the passage has sat on the page for two thousand years as a snare even to the wary.

Luther, for example, got it only mostly right. Let me quote from his gloss on Romans 6:13 and 14.

> 13. *But,* here [Paul] expounds the same idea even more clearly, *do not yield,* surrender or offer voluntarily, even though they may be so inclined, *your members as instruments, tools, of wickedness unto sin,* which is unbelief, so that they serve sin unto unrighteousness, *but yield,* present, even though your sin struggles against it, *yourselves,* your whole selves first, *to God as men who have been brought from death to life,* spiritually and humbly, living in the spirit and not in obedience to sin, but consenting to righteousness, *and your members to God as instruments,* tools and servants, *of righteousness,* which comes from faith, that they may serve God unto righteousness. And you can do this easily:
> 14. *For sin will have no dominion over you,* unless you want it to. It cannot have dominion. The reason is: *since you are not under the Law but under grace,* because you have fulfilled the Law through faith in Christ, whose righteousness and work of fulfillment is yours by the grace of a merciful God which is given to you.

That is so close to the mark that it is almost a shame to fault it. And the fault in it is really so minor that one regrets withholding the rewarding cigar. But alas, it must be withheld. For the all-important seal between the realm of morality and the realm of grace—the ethics-tight bulkhead that every Christian theologian must strive unceasingly to build—has a leak in it. Perhaps not in Luther's own mind, but certainly in the minds of those who read him. And the leak is at the word *voluntarily* in the very beginning of the passage. Left unstopped, it slowly but inevitably lets the whole subject of morality seep back in and swamp the notion of grace.

For any talk of the role of the human will in the plan of salvation invites back into the gospel of grace the purely moralistic distinction between sin and temptation—a distinction that Jesus once and for all tossed to the dogs when he said that thinking about adultery was as bad as doing it. It leads us to imagine that in the risen life of grace, while there may be all the trappings of our death, while there may be mental motions toward sin, nifty ideas of renewed tricks with old (or new) partners, *seeds* of possible sin, we are still okay—*but only as long as we can say in our heart of hearts we haven't watered the damned things and brought them to flower.*

But that is simply the old law of salvation by our own integrity, and it blows the gospel of grace to bits. In the risen life of grace, there are not just the trappings of our death, there is our death itself; not just the tinder of sin, but the full, raging fire. That is simply true. To make a distinction between the unlit tinder and the blazing inferno and then to suggest that as long as you don't get lit you're still safe, is to fly straight in the face of the Sermon on the Mount and to require not only more than human nature, even under grace, has ever been able to manage, but also more than grace itself has ever demanded. It is a case of theological imagery riding roughshod over revelation.

The gospel invites us to believe not that we are safe, *provided,* but that we are safe, *period.* It is not that sin *should not* have dominion over us, but that it *cannot,* for its power has been destroyed by Jesus. It reigns in our death, of course, as it always did, but what is that? What is it to have sway over a valley of dry bones? The main thing is that it does not reign over Jesus, and Jesus is our life.

And there is the crucial point: therefore we are safe. Not safe, *if . . .* not safe, *as long as . . .* not safe, *provided.* . . . Add anything—even a single qualifier, even a single hedge—and you lose the gospel of salvation, which is just Jesus, Jesus, Jesus.

"Ah but!" you say. "What about faith? Do we not need to trust Jesus—does not Paul need to live in faith, in fidelity to Laura, in order to reap the benefits of his safety?"

And all I can say to you when you ask me such a thing is that, even though there is a skin of reason on what you say, I must tell you no. Not because it is false, but because it is such an obvious piece of elementary blather, such a minor aspect of the major truth, that you should be ashamed to bring it up. Of course no man can enjoy an acceptance he denies. But she *died* for him, for Christ's sake! She kissed his feet, she prostrated herself under the wheels of his great, brakeless dumptruck of a life—and she did it in advance and without proviso. His faith is trash compared to that. His hope is junk compared to that. There is, of course, still love, and it is still the greatest of the three. But even Paul's love, compared to the grace by which he is saved, is hardly worth a line of type.

She died—Christ died—without waiting for him to reduce his sins to the level of temptations. "Greater love hath no man than this, that a man lay down his life for his friends." *"While we were yet sinners,* Christ died for the ungodly." To work up a theology, then, in which you hold that someone who would do a thing like that is in reality still waiting to see whether you will shape up before he goes through with what he has in mind, is simply to make chopped liver out of the mother tongue.

Once again, therefore, as the Apostle says no less than ten times in this epistle:

*Baby, there just ain't no way!*

# 15

Having disposed of our Moral Theologian Residentiary, however, we must not leap too soon to the conclusion that our grip on the doctrine of grace is now secure. You and I and Paul—all of us, let us admit it freely, persons of the more sensible sort—have probably never taken moral theology with the seriousness moral theologians think it deserves. Its straight-faced strongarm methods, its grim earnestness, its solemn insistence on the indispensibility of rules from which every man jack dispenses himself at the first inconvenience—and above all its idiotic assumption, in the face of all evidence to the contrary, that good advice will produce good behavior—is simply and unappealingly silly. *We know. We* have lectured children. *We* have told friends to use ashtrays to avoid burning holes in the sofa. *We* have asked Christians for forgiveness.

But we are not yet, for all that wisdom of experience, secure. For we—we especially—carry in our heads another Reverend Gentleman, one of an appropriately finer sort himself, whose noble blandishments, while they are vastly more commendable than the moralist's pushing and shoving, are nonetheless just as inimical to a true perception of grace. This fellow is our resident Spiritual Director, our private chaplain, our personal guru, whose forte is mucking up the doctrine of grace, not in the name of ethics but of spirituality. His speciality is not commandments but counsels of perfection.

Let me show you him at work with Paul. Let us assume, not unreasonably, that by and by (and probably sooner than later) Paul's promiscuity tapers off, that he reaches a point at which he is indeed, physically and mentally, faithful to Laura alone. I say "not unreasonably" because even though grace makes no conditions about reform, it does—and not always conveniently—produce the conditions that induce reform. Grace works our restoration the way physical life works our healing, by producing a general tilt in the direction of health, by being a force for wholeness which, while it never forces, continually disposes us to become whole.

As Augustine says, "Before grace, we had no free choice about not sinning; the best we could do was want not to sin. But grace has the effect of making us not only want to do right, but also able to do it—not by our own powers, of course, but by the help of our Liberator."

Let us assume then, that Paul has arrived at that blessed state where he is, within the limits of the admittedly different morality of this parable, a righteous man: he has one wife to whom he is attentive, duteous and kind, and one mistress whom he loves as his own life. There are just Sarah and Laura. He is a proper romantic adulterer, happily married and wildly in love.

It is at this point that his Spiritual Director sits him down for a heart-to-heart talk about his personal development. He enquires whether Paul has thought perhaps of making a little retreat. He urges him to take time to dwell on the greatness of his acceptance by Laura and on the shining newness of the life he enjoys by her. He suggests that he consider whether he has made, not a proper romantic response to her—he has indeed done that—but the fullest possible romantic response to her.

Next, he reads a few passages of Scripture to him:

> And the young man saith unto Jesus, All these commandments I have kept from my youth up. What lack I yet? Jesus said to him, If thou wilt be perfect, go and sell all that thou hast, and give to the poor, and thou shalt have treasure in heaven; and come and follow me. But when the young man heard that saying, he went away sorrowful: for he had great possessions.

> If any man come to me, and hate not his father, and mother, and wife, and children, and brethren, and sisters, yea, and his own life also, he cannot be my disciple.

> No man having put his hand to the plow, and looking back, is fit for the kingdom of heaven.

Then Paul's Private Chaplain, being of the newer, nondirective sort, leaves him to meditate in silence on the obvious question: "If I really love Laura, shouldn't I divorce Sarah?"

And Paul, entranced by the vision of spiritual perfection, goes for it like a bluefish after a tin squid. He sees that to be truly perfect, he would not only have to break with his family, but would also have to do it without putting the least pressure on Laura to do likewise. And the vision expands. He contemplates the offering of himself and looks on while the romantic Angel does wonderously and ascends in the flame of the altar. He sees himself holed up in his bachelor digs having renounced all for love, pauperized by alimony payments, with nothing but Sunday afternoon visitation rights and two weeks in August. And he weeps over the poignancy of it all; but he finally dries his eyes, squares his shoulders, takes up the cross of perfection, and phones his lawyer.

Do you know what that is from the point of view of grace? It is a lot of malarkey. It is outrageous nonsense because what he is doing is forgetting the true gospel of his salvation—Laura took him *without condition, before everything*—and inventing a false one—a gospel, not this time of salvation by moral integrity, but of salvation by poignancy and superspirituality, a gospel that says that heaven is not only for bad guys turned good, but especially for good guys who go everybody one better.

But it remains malarkey. There is no way of tying the kingdom of heaven to anything we do. It comes because the King makes it come, not because we give it a helping hand. Paul may do any stupid or brilliant thing he wants with his freedom under grace, but whatever he does, he mustn't think its worth a damn in the process of his salvation. Which is why, in my parable, Paul and Laura just do the graceful, sensible thing and stay lovers. They don't take on a lot of dumb, supererogatory vows.

The Reformers, you see, were dead right on this subject. They carried on—no, that's much too weak—they ranted and raved endlessly about the iniquity of works of supererogation, about the falseness of the notion that the gasoline of grace could be made to give better mileage if you put into it the additive of some more perfect performance.

Read Luther on the subject of clerical celibacy, for example. The Reformation was a time when men went blind, staggering drunk because they had discovered, in the dusty basement of late medievalism, a whole cellarful of 1500-year-old, 200-proof grace—of bottle after bottle of pure distillate of Scripture, one sip of which would convince anyone that God saves us single-handedly. The word of the Gospel—after all those centuries of trying to lift yourself into heaven by worrying about the perfection of your bootstraps—suddenly turned out to be a flat announcement that the saved were home free even before they started. How foolish then, they said, how reprehensibly misleading, to take the ministers of that word of free, unqualified acceptance and slap enforced celibacy on them—to make their lives bear a sticker that said they had gone an extra mile and paid an extra toll. It was simply to hide the light of grace under a bushel of pseudo-law, to take the sacrament of the mystery and go out of your way to make it look as little like the mystery as possible. And for the Reformers that was simply a crime. Grace was to be drunk neat: no water, no ice, and certainly no ginger ale; neither goodness, nor badness, nor the flowers that bloom in the spring of superspirituality could be allowed to enter into the case.

In my parable therefore (if you insist on seeing it in the tawdriest light) Paul lives at home and loves on the side. For myself, though, I would rather say that he lives at Laura and loves everywhere. Because the ultimate mischief in the doctrine of salvation by spiritual perfection is its inveterate tendency to exclusivity rather than inclusiveness, its drive to prescind rather than comprehend—in a word, its parochializing of news that can be good only as long as it is catholic. In the name of a romantic purity, it takes the lover who sings in the shower before treating his wife to a birthday dinner and tells him that the best thing he could do would be to get the hell out of his marriage. That it does its mischief under the guise of heroic generosity and total dedication is just more nonsense. The *via negativa* has its place, but not in the *effecting* of anybody's salvation. And even in its place, you have to watch it like a hawk: at the flick of a renunciation, it can turn just stingy, stingy, stingy.

So the parable stands as written: Paul and Laura and Sarah—and Catharine and Janet et al.—all stay where they are. Insofar as they live at all, it is by no devices of their own. They, and we, are dead, and our life is hid with Christ in God. We need not be covetous of crosses: there will be plenty to go around and there will be the grace that reigns over death in every one of them. We were never told it would not hurt, only that nothing would get permanently out of hand; not that it would not often go hard with us, but that *there is therefore now no condemnation to them which are in Christ Jesus.*

*      *      *

Take my yoke upon you and learn of me; for I am meek and lowly in heart: and ye shall find rest unto your souls.

For my yoke is easy, and my burden is light.

# 16

*There is therefore now no condemnation to them which are in Christ Jesus.*

I think that my parable has taken us just about as far as it can. By the very fact that it is only a fictional analogue to the dispensation of grace, it stops short of conveying to you the flat-footed reality of what the Apostle says in this ultimate proposition. It leaves you still in a merely possible world where you feel free to dawdle and dream before returning, as you see it, to the harsh realities of the daily grind.

"Ah yes," you say, "a lovely story. How nice to think of what it would be like if, in the thick of our sins, we were told that we stood uncondemned by a love that would not let us go. Thank you for diverting me; it has been a pleasure meeting you. But now, alas, I must get back to the salt mine."

By its very nature, you see, my parable has brought you to the point of missing its point altogether. St. Paul has not said to you, "Think how it would be if there were no condemnation"; he has said, "There *is* therefore now none." He had made an unconditional, not a conditional statement—a flat assertion, not a parabolic one. He has not said, "God has done this and that and the other thing, and if, by dint of imagination, you can manage to put them all together, you may be able to experience a little solace in the prison of your days." No, He has simply said, "You are free. Your services are no longer required. The salt mine has been closed."

It is essential that you see this clearly. The Apostle is saying that you, and Paul, and I have been sprung. Right now; not next week, or at the end of the world. And unconditionally, with no probation officer to report to. But that means that we have finally come face to face with the one question we have always thought we were aching to hear but that we now realize we have scrupulously ducked every time it got within a mile of us. It was the question I raised in the very first chapter, and it has been lurking all along: *What would you do with freedom if you had it?* Only now it is posed to you not in the subjunctive but in the indicative: *You are free. What do you plan to do?*

And St. Paul means really free. Free forever. And not just because the salt mine has been closed. For who knows, the local authorities might change their minds in a day or a year and reinstitute the prison system of blame and guilt. Heaven knows, they have never left it in abeyance for long in the past. No. You are free, not because they have promised not to prosecute you, but because they could not prosecute you, even if they wanted to. And for a very simple reason: you are dead. You have fallen under the ultimate statute of limitation. You are out from under everything. Law, sin, guilt, blame: it all rolls off your back like rain off a tombstone.

But—and this is the crucial point so easily missed—the Apostle says more than that. He says *you are dead to the law by the body of Christ.* Do you see what that means? It means that it is not only you who are dead and beyond the orbit of blame, but God too. God himself, the Supreme Lawgiver, Blamefixer, and Guiltspreader, has died to the whole sorry business in the death of Jesus.

There is, therefore, no condemnation for two reasons: first, there is nobody left to be condemned; and second, there is nobody around to do the condemning. And likewise, there is therefore *now* no condemnation for two reasons: you are dead now; and God, the Lamb slain from the foundation of the world, has been dead all along. The blame game was over before it started. All Jesus did was announce the truth of that and tell you it would make you free. It was admittedly a dangerous thing to do. You *are* a menace. But he did it, and therefore, menace or not, here you stand, uncondemned, forever, *now.* What are you going to do with your freedom?

*　　*　　*

I shall not, because I cannot, answer that question for you. I have enough trouble answering it for myself, so I shall just wish us both well. But, having warned you already about your Resident Moralist and your Private Chaplain, I feel I should also warn you of a third tempter who, even though you are now free in fact, will continue to work day and night to put you back in the only prison left: the prison of your own mind. I shall call her (or him—of whichever sex, this old maid is an incorrigible biddy) the Old Party.

You have known her all your conscious life. She is your Resident Gossip, and she has had your ear so long and so successfully that even though none of the superstitions and old wives' tales she has regaled you with have ever proved to be true, you still believe every word she says and tremble at the power of her tongue.

It was she who, when you were five, told you that a cut in the flap of skin between your thumb and forefinger would give you lockjaw: she left you convinced for life that at the first, slightest scratch, your bottom teeth would clang shut like a prison gate. At the age of seven she informed you that wearing rubbers indoors would draw your eyes: to this day, even in ripeness and perfectness of age, your eyes grow heavy if you keep your galoshes on in the house. At nine, she warned you that stepping on a crack would break your mother's back; at twelve, that masturbation would turn your brains to mashed potatoes and grow hair on the palms of your hands; at eighteen, that fellatio would give you fever sores; at twenty-five, that you probably had an asymptomatic case of syphilis; and at forty, that adulterers always get caught. But all along and above all, it was she who persuaded you that even if every one of these dire metaphysical linkages between your actions and her version of the constitution of the universe should somehow fail, *God would still get you in the end.*

My parable is over. But were it to continue, the Old Party would now go to work on Paul with all the resources of her big, ignorant mouth. In the face of the overarching fact of his life—his free acceptance by the grace of the beloved—she would try to talk him into functional impotence with Laura just because, at some time subsequent to his confession of death, he strays for a moment and actually acts dead—just because, in plain English, he happens to screw around again. Or she would, stealing a page from the Spiritual Director's devotional manual, try to talk him into a similar impotence with his wife on the grounds that the universe, which for years has payed no attention at all to his sex life, has suddenly set up an inexorable causal connection between Sarah and Laura.

She will, in other words, worry him with any gossip she can find about what other people think, regale him with any fairy tale she can confect from astrology, psychology, magic or religion, fill his head with whatever folk unwisdom, ancient or modern, she can lay a hand to, in order to convince him that the fictions that flourished in his death are somehow stronger than the fact that is his life. And all to one end: to get his mind—and yours, and mine—off that only fact.

Which is, of course, that we are dead and our life is hid with Christ in God. Dead. Out of the causal nexus for good. Dead. Not on trial. Dead. Out of the judicial process altogether. Not indicted, not prosecuted, not bound over, not found guilty. Just dead. And the lovely thing of it is that we were dead even before they came to get us. We have beaten the system. In Christ, we have cheated the cosmos and slipped the bonds of every necessity the Old Party will ever wave in front of us. *There is therefore now no condemnation.* It doesn't matter what the universe thinks. It doesn't matter what other people think. It doesn't matter what you think. It doesn't even matter what God thinks, because God has said he isn't going to think about it any more. All he thinks now is Jesus, Jesus, Jesus; and Jesus now is all your life. You are, therefore, free. Spit in the Old Party's eye; it's the only language she understands.

# 17

I do, however, owe you two things. The first is an admission. I grant you that I have, in this parable, been working only one side of the street—that in the effort to do justice to grace, I have neglected justice itself. And I am fully aware that in doing so, I have laid myself open to the charge of granting, not only licenses for promiscuity, but also franchises for far worse things: for pride and prejudice, for torture and exploitation—in short, for getting away with murder.

I shall say only two things in my defense. First, Scripture lays itself open to the same charge. Second, the other side of the street has been worked so long, so hard, and so often, that most people don't even know there is a sunny side. The Terrible Trio of the Moral Theologian, the Spiritual Director and the Old Party have conspired to keep the church from any prolonged and serious consideration of the doctrine of grace. Every time it is rediscovered, she sends in an army of moralizers, backwaterers and scholasticizers to get her clear of it in the shortest possible time. Bad enough that even St. Paul, even Augustine, even Luther should have retrenched, however slightly, on their insights into grace; simply abysmal, though, that their assigns and devisees, in less time than it took to compose a *commentarium,* almost invariably put the subject into total eclipse. We hate and fear freedom, in spite of all our lip service to it. My parable stands therefore without apology. It's just my ten-cent contribution to liberty's sadly impoverished eternal vigilance fund.

But second, I owe you something more. I have expounded St. Paul to you as saying that not only are *we* dead to sin, but that God is dead to it too—that he has put himself out of commission on the whole subject of blame. And so, indeed, he has: "I will forgive their iniquity and I will remember their sin no more."

I am fully aware that the Scriptures are paradoxical—that God speaks with a forked tongue—and that every lovely thing he says on the side of leniency can be matched by a dozen stringencies that will curl your hair. But I am also convinced that every man has to make a decision about such utterances. When someone tells you all kinds of things about his attitude toward you, you must first look at him long and long, and decide for yourself whether you care about him at all. But if you then come to the conclusion that you do, you must decide which of his words you will take as his *governing word.*

You ask me why I think God's leniency governs his severity? Why grace is his sovereign attribute? Well, all I can say to you is that, having been a father who has spoken out of both sides of his mouth to eight children for 32 years—and having all those years believed in a heavenly Father who saved us, not by sitting in his penthouse issuing edicts, but by sending us the warm, furry body of a Son who drank the nights away with us and died obscurely of the foolishness of it all—all I can say is that I put my bet on the left fork of the tongue. It is my best hope that, when my children think of everything I have said and done to them, they choose to remember the times of my severity when I just gave them a kiss on the cheek, poured myself a Scotch, and shut up. And it is my last hope that God hopes the same for himself.

So I really do make no apology for landing on the sunny side of the street. I am sorry if I have offended you, but to me there are some things that simply override everything that comes before or after; and I am sorrier still if you do not feel the same way. For without that ultimate *cassation*—without that final quashing of the subpoena, that throwing of the prosecution's case out of court that is the only music there is to the ears of the hopelessly guilty—you and I, Virginia, are simply sunk.

So what I owe you in the second place is some vision that will stir your imagination to go where your mind and your emotions and your history—and those three dreadful parasites in your head—have conspired for years to keep you from going; some image that will enable you to figure to yourself what that final cassation might be like; some picture to suggest at least one way in which God might avoid his own unavoidable justice, might know the enslaving truth about you, and yet refuse to keep you bound; some scene that will convince at least your heart that you are free.

Imagine with me, therefore, two lovers in bed. Paul and Laura will do nicely, although this isn't about them any more: it is about the two Ultimate Lovers, God the Father and God the Son—and about the Third Ultimate Lover, God the Holy Spirit, the Divine Us, who proceeds forth from their loving. Still, think of the Father and the Son, if you will, as a man and a woman in a motel from noon till three.

(I am aware that the switching of the Son's gender may make some of the natives restless. They could solve the problem for themselves of course, by thinking of all the passages where God the Son, the creating Word, is referred to in the feminine gender—where he is presented under the image of the *Wisdom* of God: the *Sapientia Dei* that mightily and sweetly orders all things, the *Hagia Sophia* that was with him from the beginning—where he is called, in short, *Saint Sophie*. Or, alternatively, I could solve it for them by making the lovers homosexuals; but I have a feeling that might make them even more restless than two heterosexuals in a Holiday Inn. Let it pass.)

Laura told Paul she remembered reading somewhere that in the order of nature place creates persons, but that in the order of grace persons create place. One of the perennial problems of theology is how to imagine, how to figure to ourselves, the way in which God, having made the world and let it get out of whack, manages to get it back in shape. The problem is usually solved by thinking of God as coming down from heaven and fixing something: putting in a new fuse or doing a valve job on the world so it will run right again.

But that introduces an impossible set of images. It suggests that God is, in his deepest being, at some distance from the world, and that, if he turns up at all, he comes as a kind of celestial road service doing incidental repairs after the damage has been done. However, if there is indeed therefore *now* no condemnation, it can mean only one thing: that from the most important point of view (God's), he was already there before the damage was done, and he fixed it before it had a chance to do any damage.

Because if God can tell you that *now* you are uncondemned for some sin you are committing right now or even will commit next week (and he does indeed tell you just that), then he's talking about something a lot more intimate to your being than some *ex post facto* visit by a garage mechanic. He is talking about something he is present to eternally. He is telling you that as far as his Word is concerned (and his Word *goes*), you have never been out of line at all—or, more accurately, that anything you may have put out of line was, in the very moment of its misalignment, realigned then and there by the suave and forceful *Wisdom* that goes through all things and is more moving than any motion. And above all he is telling you that what was announced in Jesus by that Word, what was done in Jesus by that Wisdom, was not the temporal start of the repair of your wreck, but the final accomplishment of it from the beginning by the Lamb slain from the foundation of the world—by the Ultimate Beloved whose voice creates and reconciles all.

Put that together, therefore, and ask the right question. Do not ask, "Where is God, and how does he get here, and what does he do when he arrives?" Ask instead, "Where is the world?"

And then you finally see. The world is in bed with Paul and Laura, with the Father and Saint Sophie. The world leaps out of nothing into being between the lips of the Word and the ear of the Father. The world is what the Ultimate Beloved whispers to the Ultimate Lover. Creation is the Pillow Talk of the Trinity. The world is the Place the Divine Persons create by the power of their eternal Affair.

Do you see now? Do you see why, in that bed, *there can be nothing wrong?* Why you are uncondemned and free, just by being? It is because, if the Wisdom of God be for you, nothing can be against you, nothing can separate you from the love of Christ. For you are the very body of that love and if Wisdom speaks you into being in that bed, she speaks you reconciled forever. Whatever in you is evil, or nasty, or stupid, or sad is not mentioned in that bed; it is taken down into the Silence of the Word which is the Forgetting of the Father. Laura unspeaks the unspeakableness that is Paul and makes all things new. She takes into herself his condemnation and sequesters it in the stillness of her own gracious death. And the world she creates in his ear is the peaceable kingdom. Within the limits of my parable, it is the one place where he really lives. And outside those limits—in the Land of the Trinity itself, in the Bed where Wisdom murmurs in the Father's ear—it is the only place where we exist at all. And all that is there, and all that there is, is love and laughter and the joy of having gotten away with everything. "Behold thou art fair, my beloved, yea, pleasant: also our bed is green. The beams of our house are cedar, and our rafters of fir."

Do you see then finally why there is no condemnation *now?* It is because there never was any—because there is nothing more sovereign than the sovereignty of grace. If you are still so committed to working the other side of the street that you want room for hell in that bed, I can give it to you. But I will not give it here, because hell is nothing but a vain fornication of fancy in the presence of the love that will not let you go. In the end, it is only for forsaking; and the price of the forsaking is exactly nothing. To be at all, is to be in that Bed; and to be in that Bed is to be free. That is where, and what, you have been all along: you are, therefore, at liberty. You may *go.*

*      *      *

I know I cannot prove all that. But since it *is* what the man said, and since it sounds so much better than anything else I have ever been told—since, of all the tired truths I know, it comes closer than any to sounding like the hilarity beyond all liking and happening—I just chuckle to myself and try my best to believe it. I urge you to do the same. After all, you weren't really dying to hear *bad* news, were you?

*There is therefore now no condemnation to them which are in Christ Jesus.*

      ... It is not easy
To believe in unknowable justice
    Or pray in the name of a love
Whose name one's forgotten: *libera*
    *Me, libera* C (dear C)
And all poor s-o-b's who never
    Do anything properly, spare
Us in the youngest day when all are
    Shaken awake, facts are facts,
(And I shall know exactly what happened
    Today between noon and three)
That we, too, may come to the picnic
    With nothing to hide, join the dance
As it moves in perichoresis,
    Turns about the abiding tree.

## PART II

# Coffee Hour

# 18

I know. Once again, I have overstated things slightly—this time perhaps even more than slightly. But since my story did at least succeed in separating the liquor of grace from the mash of morality, let the question of style pass. Besides, there are still differences of substance between us and I have (I admit it) papered them over with a kind of theological throwaway that inspires less than confidence in your mind. You deserve better before we make an end. I shall try again, therefore, and by another device.

\*　　　\*　　　\*

When I preach a sermon that finally succeeds in going to the root of the idea of redemption by grace alone, I find that those who take it in have two successive but opposite reactions. One Sunday, to give you an instance, I set myself the task of showing that in the parables of grace, the work of redemption is done entirely by the redeemer and not at all by the redeemed. The longer I proceeded by straight exposition, however, the more I felt that the very parables I was dealing with were keeping my hearers from seeing the truth in its naked glory. I could almost hear them worrying the tiny bones of good works in the stories rather than feasting on the meat of grace which was the main ingredient—paying more attention, for example, to the prodigal's confession than to the father's love that forgave him before he confessed; giving more weight to the minor point that the laborers who worked only one hour did at least some work, than to the main truth that the Lord of the vineyard paid everybody out of his own goodness and not at all in proportion to the work done. My mind hunted for some clinching illustration that would make them drop the irrelevancies and get on with the meal. Finally, it came:

"All right," I said. "Take it another way. I will show exactly what you have to do to be saved—the full extent of what you, personally, must undertake in order to be drawn into the redeeming work of Jesus. Put yourself in the scene in the eleventh chapter of John where Jesus is about to raise Lazarus from the dead. You are standing there next to Martha, outside the sealed tomb, and you hear Jesus say, 'Take away the stone.' But Martha objects. She says something which, if I had thought of it earlier, I would have made the text for this whole sermon. She says, 'Lord, by this time he stinketh, for he hath been dead four days.' But Jesus makes them open the tomb anyway, and after he prays to his Father, he cries with a loud voice, 'Lazarus, come forth.' And he that was dead comes blinking out into the sunlight.

"Do you now see what you have to do to be saved? Do you at last understand the precise degree of cooperation on your part needed to enable you to enter into life? Do you finally recognize that all that is required of you is to do exactly what Lazarus did—which is exactly and only *nothing?* Martha spoke the whole truth, not only about Lazarus, but about every one of us in particular and about the human race in general: 'Lord, by now we stink.' We have been dead four days, four thousand days, four hundred thousand times four thousand days. In the midst of all our life we have been in death. And in the midst of that abiding death we have been in Nothing. Knee-deep in it, waist-deep in it, up to our noses and in over our heads in Not-a-Thing. But now, in Lazarus, you see it is just that extremity that has always been our hope, that very prison, the doorway to our liberty. Because making things jump out of nothing is God's favorite act. He creates us out of it and he raises us up from it. Jesus came to raise the dead. Not to improve the improvable, not to perfect the perfectible, but to raise the dead. He never met a corpse that didn't sit right up then and there. And he never meets us without bringing us out of nothing into the joy of his resurrection: you, me, the President of the United States and poor old Arthur down by the docks with his pint of Muscatel in a brown paper bag. We are all dead. And he raises us all. And without so much as a by-your-leave. Just be a good corpse and he does the rest. Because his Word is the Word with the ultimate bark and when he says, 'Arthur, come forth,' that's all old Arthur needs. His nothin' ain't nothin' no more."

As I said, when I preach something like that I get two reactions. At the end of the sermon, I see smiles. I see faces light up—faces that, in spite of a lifetime's exposure to the doctrine of grace, seem for the first time to dare to hope that maybe there isn't a catch to it after all, that even out of the midst of their worst shipwrecks they are still going home free for the pure and simple reason that Jesus calls them. I see barely restrained hilarity at the sudden perception that he really meant it when he said his yoke was easy.

But after the service, in the time it takes everyone to get downstairs to the coffee hour, the smiles have been replaced by frowns. Their fear of the catch has caught up with them again and they surround the messenger of hope and accuse me of making the world unsafe for morality.

I propose, therefore, that you and I stop our progress at this point and do justice to the frowning, coffee-hour mood my parable of grace has put you in. It is your turn to speak. Let me now, cup in hand and sugar and cream stirred in, silence for a while my proper voice and bespeak, if I can, your words as you hold me at bay in this musty basement where the Word provokes us to dialogue.

\*       \*       \*

Oh, yes indeed (I hear you say). Speak we will. We have sat patiently through your parable about two unlikely and, we might add, unlikeable people who, in the midst of a major shipwreck of responsibility, have achieved the distinctly minor triumph of overlooking one or two of each other's unappealing features. It is not simply, though, that we resent the rather shady success of their affair. We are as fond as anyone of stories of love and grace triumphant. What we object to, to begin with, is the outrage to common moral sense with which you tried to lard the otherwise dry meat of your parable.

Why, for example, did you insist on providing Paul and Laura with wife and husband, respectively? Why could they not have been presented to us as single and therefore marriageable? We might even—our sensibilities are sufficiently modern—have settled for your leaving them unmarried lovers, if you felt that a touch of salaciousness would pique our interest. But this heavy-handed over-salting is unpardonable, precisely because it is unnecessary. You intended a happy ending for them from the start. Why could it not have been an inoffensively happy one, rather than this adulterous tangle of broken promises, this shabby, car-switching, phone-calling institutionalization of delinquency that you insist we accept as a paradigm of grace?

After all, it was not as if you were laboring under the restraints of reportage. Your story was a fiction over which you had full control. You could have brought Paul's sins to Laura's forgiveness just as well without the added offense of infidelity. We would have thought that a theologian concerned to restore our taste for the goodness of grace would compose parables less likely to set our teeth on edge.

On the other hand and much more to the point, if you were so determined to outrage our sensibilities, why were you so pusillanimous in your choice of outrages? Why did you pick such a mild one as illicit sex? We suspect we know the answer. Was it not that, having made no serious attempt to deal with the just demands of the moral order, you instinctively shied away from any clear delineation of the chamber of horrors your one-sided story opens?

You tell us, in effect, that even in the sowing of wild oats, grace springs triumphant. Why then did you provide your characters—we can quote Auden as well as you— with strains of oats of such an unmitigatedly minor wildness? Why did you not give us a Paul who deep-sixes his wife and absconds with the college endowment funds to some Caribbean country with which the United States has no extradition treaty? Why not a Laura who joins him there after lacing her husband's anniversary glass of Amaretto with prussic acid? It was not simply that you lacked inventiveness. That might be pardoned. It was that you lacked the courage to put what you were saying in words of one syllable. Your unpardonable offense, therefore, is that you have trifled with us. We are free, you claim, to do *anything*. Why did you shrink from all but the most titillating fictionalization of that freedom?

Even supposing, however, that it was not cowardice on your part—that you can still somehow, in the further explication of your thesis, make the very reconciliation of grace and the moral order for which your parable cries out—have you not made a major tactical blunder in omitting that reconciliation from the parable itself? We grant you that the theology of grace has suffered gross neglect, that we have reached a point at which almost all people, inside as well as outside the church, find that the notion of grace stands in contradiction to everything they understand by religion. But precisely because that is the case, are you not expecting too much of most readers when you ask them to learn a theology that must offend their admittedly deficient Christianity from a story that will inevitably shock their not so deficient moral sense? Might not the result be neither agreement nor disagreement, but simply misunderstanding?

Specifically, when you exegete your parable as you go along, and do so in an age which has come to believe that salvation consists in getting rid of hangups—that every easing of the psyche, however inconvenient to others, is *ipso facto* the Will of God—will you not be thought to do no more than approve of successful adulteries, or even perhaps, setting aside that particularly attractive dereliction, to advance the popular but mindless proposition that a person may do anything that comes into his head, as long as he can work himself around to the point at which it doesn't upset his insides? As Chesterton pointed out, that justifies feeding babies to crocodiles, if you have the stomach for it.

Permit us to press the point further. We are not saying that your parable is without redeeming features. We welcome the life you have given to a number of truths that need resurrection just now. We enjoyed especially your diverting us back to a better understanding of the pivotal theological concepts of law and death and repentance and grace. But we are left still with a deep conviction that your chosen theological method—your decision, as you put it, to work only one side of the street—is fundamentally suspect.

Take, for example, the master text of St. Paul to which you so often appeal. In the first eight chapters of the Epistle to the Romans, not only does he present the truth of grace as inseparable from the truth of the law, he follows it, four short chapters later, with a veritable compendium of moral theology whose exhortations to putting off the works of darkness and walking honestly as in the day, whose prohibitions of chambering and wantonness consist ill, to put it mildly, with the furtive motel-hopping of your protagonists. (We spare you further detail, assuming you to be well aware of the fact that in the immediately following Epistle, I Corinthians, St. Paul enunciates a standard of sexual morality that would not only put a crimp in Paul's and Laura's style, but would require their excommunication on the spot as fornicators).

It is not our purpose, however, to cite chapter and verse against you, only to observe how different a tissue from St. Paul you present: one hundred seventy pages of yours on half a paradox, as against fourteen of his on the full width of the fabric of truth. One of our number remarked somewhat facilely that every major heretic has cut his teeth on the Epistle to the Romans. We reject that as an adequate assessment but feel it contains a timely warning to you. The essence of heresy is not that it propounds error, but that it serves up parts of the truth in the absence of those other parts without which truth cannot be kept whole. Have you not, in spite of all your demurrers, come perilously close to just such a lapse from catholicity? Even Augustine—even Luther—did not find it necessary to stand so far from one side of St. Paul in order to exegete the other.

For the time being, though, let us stop there. Reserving our right of rejoinder at some further point in the discussion, we ask you now to answer us in as plain and earnest a way as we have questioned you. We are by no means unteachable. It is just that we wish to be sure that it is truth, and not snake oil, you are asking us to buy.

# 19

*Dear me. Snake oil, indeed! This threatens to become a coffee hour and a half.*

If I assess your thoughts correctly (I now cease to bespeak your mind and return to the effort to express my own), the counts against me can be reduced to five particulars. It is your contention that I have

1. outraged your moral sense but, at the same time,
2. insufficiently outraged your moral sense, and thus
3. been guilty of trifling with you;
4. made no serious attempt to deal with the just demands of the moral order, and
5. opened the door to a purely subjective morality.

On then with the defense.

      *            *            *

I pass the catch-22 formulation you have given the first three of your charges (Outrage, Insufficient Outrage, and Trifling) and go to the central and serious matter that lies behind them. The crime you are actually accusing me of is *healing on the sabbath.* I shall be as succinct as possible.

To begin with, a delineation of its essence. The crime always consists of three elements: first, the doing of a good deed; second, the doing of that deed in a way that violates a deeply felt ethical sensibility; and third, the doing of it before people to whom the violation seems not only unnecessary, but also destructive of an entire tissue of values. It is invariably seen as blasphemy and its punishment, allowing for minor variation in time or circumstance, must always be death. Properly understood, it is the crime of crimes. Nevertheless, fully aware that a plea of guilty is equivalent to conviction after trial, I do so plead myself.

I ask you only to see what I have done against the background of the Gospels. In the twelfth chapter of Matthew, Jesus, in a synagogue on the sabbath day, heals a man who has a withered hand. Promptly, and quite correctly, the Pharisees go out and hold a council against him, how they might destroy him. Notice, in order of ascending importance, the three elements of the crime.

First, Jesus does an unquestionably good deed. Next, he does it in front of people whom he knows perfectly well to be committed to the whole body of the law—and for whom the keeping of the sabbath is no trifle but one of the supreme sacraments of the law, an affirmation (if you take Genesis 1:1–2:3 at face value) of the whole divine order of creation. But third, his breaking of the sabbath seems pointless and unnecessary. He is not performing a good deed that, if delayed, would become unperformable. This is not a man who needs immediate rescue, not a man lying unconscious in a burning house. This is not even a man whose case is like the one Jesus cites to justify the healing—a sheep fallen into a pit who would drown if left till sundown. The Pharisees are reasonable men. Of course they would pull out the sheep. If you care to make a rather Latin-style theological argument for them, you might have them reason that since the sabbath is the chief sacrament of the order of creation, it may lawfully be broken only if some significant individual instance of that order is in danger of imminent and irreversible disordering.

But that is not the case here. This man has had a withered hand for years. Why in God's good name can't Jesus wait out the afternoon and cure him without flying in the face of the Torah? Why can't he sit with him till sunset and use the time to fix the man's mind on the graciousness of God? Why can't they search the Scriptures together and set the stage so that the healing will be seen in all its unquestionable rightness? What is the point of this unnecessary muddying of the water?

In order to see it you have to go back. The point that Jesus had in mind was the point he made earlier the same day when the Pharisees caught him and his disciples going through the corn plucking off ears and eating them: the Son of Man is Lord even of the sabbath day. It is for the Pharisees not only a new point, but one that is at odds with all the other points they accept. And, while it is not the same point as the one made in my parable, Jesus' method of making it—the dynamic he uses to put it before their minds—is the same, I think, as the one I have used to put the truth of grace before yours. Consider.

Whenever someone attempts to introduce a radically different insight to people whose minds have been formed by an old and well-worked-out way of thinking, he is up against an obstacle. Their taste, as Jesus said, for the old wine is so well established that they invariably prefer it to the new. More than that, the new wine, still fermenting, seems to them so obviously and dangerously full of power that they will not even consider putting it into their old and fragile wineskins.

But try to see the point of the biblical imagery of wine-making a little more abstractly. The new insight is always at odds with the old way of looking at things. Even if the teacher's audience were to try earnestly to take it in, the only intellectual devices they have to pick it up with are the categories of the old system with which it conflicts. Hence the teacher's problem: if he leaves in his teaching a single significant scrap of the old system, their minds, by their very effort to understand, will go to that scrap rather than to the point he is making and, having done that, will understand the new only insofar as it can be made to agree with the old—which is not at all.

Perhaps the phrase "precluding the conversion of species in an argument" will do for a name for this teaching technique that Jesus uses in healing on the sabbath, and that I have used in presenting you with grace in the context of an adultery. Were Jesus to have waited till sundown to heal the man's hand, the minds of the Pharisees would have seen his good deed as congruent with everything else they already knew. If, then, they were to try to put a messianic interpretation on it, they would envision Jesus as the kind of messiah they were ready for—a victorious and immortal one—and not as the kind he knew himself to be, a suffering and dying one.

He was at pains, you see, to present them with a proposition that was totally unacceptable to them: that the kind of Christ he was must suffer, and die, and on the third day rise again. The species of his argument, if you will, was that he would be a different messiah than they expected. He must not, therefore, offer their minds illustrations that allow them to convert the species into its opposite. If he heals after sundown, the very goodness of that act—the very legitimacy they attach to it—will seep back and erode his main point: they will acclaim him only as the long-awaited man on horseback who is coming to punch the enemies of the Lord in the nose.

Note too, please, that this precluding of the conversion of species is no merely incidental device of Jesus'; it is his chief method. He comes from Galilee, whence arises no messiah; his disciples are a ragtag lot of outcasts, likewise from Galilee; he consorts with a Samaritan woman; he eats with publicans and sinners; he is a glutton and a winebibber; and he dies accursed, hung on a tree. He constantly couches his announcement of the kingdom in words and deeds that are at odds with his hearers' expectations for the kingdom, precisely in order that seeing they might not see and hearing they might not understand. He instructs them with a constant awareness that the one thing they must not do is see, because they would see wrong, nor understand, because they would only misunderstand. For he knows that the only thing that can save them—himself, in the mystery of his death and resurrection—is the one thing they cannot accept on their present view of salvation. Accordingly, he gives them not one scrap to confirm their present view—or, more accurately, he always includes one solidly unacceptable scrap on which their minds will gag.

This long footnote to my plea of guilty, therefore, begins to draw to an end. My parable gave you one good deed: Laura's acceptance of Paul. It gave it to you in a way that outraged your ethical sensibilities (whether the outrage was sufficient or insufficient hardly matters: it outraged you; that is enough). And it did so in a way that seemed both unnecessary and destructive of values (it trifled, as you said, with people concerned to uphold important truths). It is indeed, therefore, healing on the sabbath.

But I did it all to preclude the conversion of the species of grace into the species of law. For the happy, innocuous ending you want would inevitably do just that. The very congruence of it with the law would wash away your perception of the point I was making. Paul and Laura respectably married? Why that would make you see grace as a way back to the sovereignty of the law—grace as a mere one- or two-shot remission of guilt whose chief purpose was to suspend the rules for a while and give a second chance to people who now, having run out of chances, had best get back to the business that God really has in mind for them, namely, minding their p's and q's.

For at the roots of our fallen being that is what we really think. Our pride drives us to establish our own righteousness. We strive all our life to see ourselves as keepers of rules we cannot keep, as loyal subjects of laws under which we can only be judged outlaws. Yet so deep is our need to derive our identity from our own self-respect—so profound is our conviction that unless we watch our step, the watchbird will take away our name—that we will spend a lifetime trying to do the impossible rather than, in one carefree minute, consent to having it done for us by someone else.

Were I to have married Paul and Laura, your mind would have come to rest in the eventual legitimacy of their relationship and not in the grace that was its only root. For Paul—and you and I—remain permanently illegitimate. We need more than occasional suspensions of the rules. We need grace. And grace is not the offer of an exception to the rules; it is a new dispensation entirely. It says nothing about the rules (indeed, it leaves them intact); it simply says that since, by our weakness, the rules can never be the *basis of our acceptance*, God is not going to make them such any more.

Accordingly, in my view, there is nothing in my presentation of grace via a story of two people who have excused themselves from the received sexual ethic that is not, with minor changes or perhaps even with none at all, in Jesus' presentation of himself as a sabbath-breaking messiah. I am guilty as charged, and I find myself in very good company indeed.

*     *     *

On the other hand, when it comes to your last two charges (*No Seriousness about the Just Demands of the Moral Order; Fostering a Purely Subjective Morality*) I feel I must plead myself not guilty, with an explanation.

I think I have answered your question about why I put no reconciliation of grace and the moral order within my parable itself. Let me take up these charges, then, by commenting on your assertion that my parable, under the guise of titillation, opens a chamber of horrors in which it is just to feed babies to crocodiles, provided only that you like that sort of thing.

You seem to imply that I, by titillating—or, more seriously, God by being gracious—run the risk of giving the impression that there is no longer any objective law against anything. Let us make some distinctions. If you mean that there are people utterly committed to doing evil who are waiting for either me or God to give them permission to proceed with their wicked designs, I deny your point. Monumental wickedness just doesn't work that way. It is always clever enough to convince itself that it is not breaking the law, but keeping some higher law—

that it needs no permission to destroy the Jews, for example, because it is, in its own view, doing the cosmic order a favor.

If you mean, however, that there are people with an itch to do something immoral who might draw from my parable—or from the Scriptures, I might add—encouragement to scratch, I concede it. Shaky wickedness—the unsure malevolence of weak and fearful characters—always works that way. They will hunt for permission high and low until they find it, because they are engaged in an endless struggle to think well of themselves by believing that some authority thinks they are not a menace. That is the principle of their lives. They cannot act on their own without permission; but, by that very fact, they will discover permission whether it is there or not because they need it like air itself. We are all used by them. If they have taken comfort from me, it is no more than they would have taken from someone else without me.

But if, on the other hand, you mean that they are going to get from my parable—or from the grace of God—serious encouragement to believe that the just demands of the moral order have been abrogated, I disagree entirely. Even if I trifle with those demands in a fiction; even if God, by his grace, is willing to put them at risk by accepting us despite our transgressions, there is simply no way of coming to a serious conclusion that morality has been set aside. The law remains the standard of our nature. To be what the law says we are is the only way we can be what we really are. No one breaks it with impunity because, by every transgression, we and the society in which we live become progressively and perceivably less human.

But for all that, no matter how far below the level of

our true humanity we sink, we retain some vision, however clouded, of what that humanity is. The law stands before us forever as a vision of the beauty of our nature: in most instances, we go on wishing that we ourselves could have kept it; and in all instances we are fully convinced that our neighbors should have kept it. The few pleasant delinquencies for which we manage to fake out permission remain just that: few.

The law against feeding babies to crocodiles, therefore, stands. I cannot topple it, and God doesn't. But there is no law that stands against God's acceptance of those who break it, *should God choose, by his own devices, to accept them.* The gospel is simply the once-for-all announcement that God has indeed so chosen.

*While we were yet sinners,* Christ died for the ungodly. It is he who reconciles me, not the law; for the law, by its very truth, shows me only that I am unreconciled. My many transgressions in the past, permitted or not—and my many transgressions in the future, including perhaps the founding of a cult that feeds babies to crocodiles—stand against me. But the gospel of grace says that God does not stand against me, that he is not and never will be my enemy, and that he has so arranged things by the mystery of Christ's death and resurrection that at any time, before, during, or after any of my sins, past or future, I can come to him just for the coming and find myself forgiven.

Do you see that what that says is far more shocking than even the worst shock I may have given you—that it means that I may well be wicked at any time, but that I am free for all time of any condemnation for my wickedness? And that therefore I am free to be wicked, monumentally or shakily, alone or with others, in thought, word or deed and with no limits upper or lower my whole life long, *and still remain free of my wickedness?* Was there any way I could have told that truth without some shock to people's systems? Indeed I begin only just now to see the validity of your point about insufficient outrageousness. The almost universal failure to grasp the gospel of grace leads me to think you may have been right. It is not exactly that my parable trifles with people, but it does perhaps overentertain them. It makes the mistake of spoon-feeding them a delicately poached filet of good news, when what they need is to have the entire uncooked fish rammed down their throats.

One footnote. If we are ever to enter fully into the glorious liberty of the sons of God, we are going to have to spend more time thinking about freedom than we do. The church, by and large, has had a poor record of encouraging freedom. She has spent so much time inculcating in us the fear of making mistakes that she has made us like ill-taught piano students: we play our songs, but we never really hear them because our main concern is not to make music but to avoid some flub that will get us in dutch. She has been so afraid we will lose sight of the laws of our nature that she has made us care more about how we look than about who we are—made us act more like the subjects of a police state than fellow citizens of the saints.

I have raised (nearly—my nail-biting days are not quite over) eight children. After some thirty years, I think all our fears that the moral order was in imminent danger of dropping out of sight were misplaced. We have spent that third of a century doing little else than wave it in front of each other's noses. My lectures to them on truthfulness were more than balanced by their tirades against me about fairness. But all the while, the one thing we needed most even then—and certainly will need from here on out into the New Jerusalem—was the ability to take our freedom seriously and act on it; to live, not in fear of mistakes, but in the knowledge that no mistake can hold a candle to the love that draws us home. My repentance, accordingly, is not so much for my failings, but for the two-bit attitude toward them by which I made them more sovereign than grace. Grace—the imperative to hear the music, not just listen for errors—makes all infirmities occasions of glory. I rest my case for Paul's and Laura's shortcomings on Rosina Lhévinne's retort to the charge that Arthur Rubinstein played wrong notes: "Yes, but *what* wrong notes!" *O felix culpa.*

*     *     *

I know, I know. The happy note I just struck probably upsets you more than anything I've said so far. Evil, you want to tell me, is no smiling matter; infirmities, be they physical or moral, are horrid before they're glorious. Where do I get off larking my way through the gravity of sin?

Well, if you like, I shall apologize for having what is on most days a sunny disposition and for deliberately avoiding the dark side of the street whenever I can. Nonetheless, I think that in omitting the horror of evil from my parable, I have done so for perfectly sound reasons. My story was an apologia for the doctrine of grace. Like any canny apologist, I tried, within the limits of a working honesty, to present my subject in the best light. Because grace is always a shock, I had to shock you; but in the interest of not losing you altogether, I chose to shock you in a motel room rather than in a death camp.

I admit that such a way of doing business does not fit the requirements of total honesty. But then, total honesty is not one of the options available to the Christian apologist. The ultimate Christian position on the horror of evil is so outrageous that even people who have bought the bill of goods can hardly accept it. No one trying to make a sale dares even mention it, especially to those whose experience of that horror has put them on the dark side of the street. Let me, therefore, lay aside my apologist's bag of tricks for one paragraph and say, as a plain Christian man, what you quite rightly fear I really mean.

There is indeed no horror, no wickedness, no evil — no cruelty, no torture, no holocaust in the whole history of the world—that is not, by the sovereignty of grace and the universality of death, reconciled already in Jesus. And there is no perpetrator of any horror, wickedness, or evil who is not by those same two facts forgiven in Jesus. That is the gospel, the good news without which, obviously, we are all dead ducks. But it is also, from where we sit, the most outrageous piece of bad news the world has ever heard: it says quite clearly that, on the basis of anything we can know or feel about the goodness of creation, God doesn't give even as much of a damn about it as we do— and that therefore he himself is no damn good.

All I can say is that I know and feel that too, and I only *believe* in a God who asks me to trust his Word to the contrary in Jesus crucified and risen. Even with a sunny disposition, I can buy that only about half the time; if you cannot buy it at all, I understand. So much, then, for the total honesty of faith. Back to the comforts of theological dialogue.

More coffee, anyone?

# 20

Perhaps the best way for us to continue would be by way of question and answer. May I suggest, too, that before anyone puts a question, he introduce himself briefly? That way we'll all be able to have some sense of the context out of which the question comes and so a better appreciation of its force. Nothing too revealing, of course. Just a few lines for us to read between. Who'll be first? Ah, good! Sheila Grinch. Sheila?

"Yes. My name is Sheila Grinch. I have three girls, fifteen, twelve and nine. My husband commutes.

"What I'm afraid of in what you're saying, Father, is that people are going to get the idea it's perfectly all right to do anything they want. I mean, I know it's important to talk about grace and all, and I'm sure we need it; but there have to be some limits somewhere, don't there, or else people will just go right on lowering their standards like they always have, I guess, but especially now with all this permissiveness. It's not an easy thing, you know, to raise three young girls in this day and age what with pot all over the schools and people thinking they can sleep with just anybody and, even if they don't, acting as if they had a perfect right to stay out till all hours no matter what their parents say or how much they worry. I mean, won't they?"

Well, Sheila, I can think of a couple of answers to your question. Let me start with them and then go on to something that lies behind them.

You're worried about permissiveness—about the way the preaching of grace seems to say it's okay to do all kinds of terrible things as long as you just walk in afterward and take the free gift of God's forgiveness.

The first thing I think you have to say is that while you and I may be worried about seeming to give permission, Jesus apparently wasn't. He wasn't afraid of giving the prodigal son a kiss instead of a lecture, a party instead of probation; and he proved that by bringing in the elder brother at the end of the story and having him raise pretty much the same objections you do. He's angry about the party. He complains that his father is lowering standards and ignoring virtue—that music, dancing and a fatted calf are, in effect, just so many permissions to break the law. And to all that Jesus has the father say only one thing: "Cut that out! We're not playing good boys and bad boys any more. Your brother was dead and he's alive again. The name of the game from now on is resurrection, not bookkeeping."

The next thing is that when you say grace gives people permission to commit sins, you have to be very clear about what you mean. The statement needs some distinguishing. It seems to me that when I commit sin, I don't ask anyone to give me permission; I just take it. If what you're saying is that preaching grace might lead some people to do more of that, I suppose you're right.

But that's not a *use* of the doctrine of grace, it's an *abuse*. Grace doesn't make evil good. The law about what's right and wrong comes out of our nature as God creates it. Therefore, the law is from God. He never changes his mind about what's best for us. It's just that when we don't do what's best for us, he promises not to let the *what* force him into throwing away the *us*. He doesn't back away from the law; but when push comes to shove, as it always does with us, he makes his first rule grace.

The Bible, you see, makes a distinction between two things we sometimes confuse. They're both true, just as apples and oranges are both true, but they have different rules and mustn't be mixed up. I've been calling them what the Scripture calls them: law and grace. Let's switch to other terms and call them *edification* and *rescue:* edification meaning the process of building things up to run the way they should, and rescue meaning the process of saving them when they don't. Once you do that you can see that the two processes are always the same in the eyes of the builder/rescuer, but very often opposed in the eyes of anybody else.

Suppose this village had an absolutely infallible fire department, one that always put out every fire before it did any real damage and that never failed to save people from death or even injury. Now in the eyes of the fire department, its rescue operations are directed to the very same end as all the building operations in the village: keeping the place the way it ought to be. As a matter of fact, it's so committed to that goal that it sends out fire inspectors to make sure people are not storing oily rags in closets and to teach them all the other rules of fire-safe housekeeping.

But when the siren goes off and it turns out that the fire is in Mr. Smith's sloppy paint shop that has been cited for violations twenty times and that has caught fire three times in the past week, what do they do? Do they drive up in front of Mr. Smith's and read him the list of violations? Do they say, "We're sorry, Mr. Smith, but you have done this once too often, and we're going to have to let your place burn down, preferably with you trapped inside"? Of course they don't. They put out the fire any way they can because, in their eyes, rescue is their first business.

But what about in other people's eyes? What about in Mr. Smith's eyes, to start with? He's a pretty unreliable character apparently. Isn't all this unlimited rescuing going to encourage him in his careless ways? Isn't what he really needs a good dose of the fear of fire? The answer could very well be yes to both questions.

And what about his upright and fire-fearing neighbors? They spend time and money to make their places of business fire-safe. Isn't it unfair to them, after they have shelled out for their own safety, to be taxed just so Smith the cheapskate can have his menace of an establishment saved over and over again? Again, very likely yes.

Well, you see the point. From anybody's point of view but the fire department's, rescue can be seen as and taken for permission. But it isn't. End of subject. (You can make the same point with the illustration of an infallible lifeguard: the knowledge that rescue is guaranteed can and does lead idiots to go out in surf nobody should swim in. But the lifeguard can't let that consideration interfere with his rescuing). In other words, people may *take* permission, but the rescuer never *gives* it. Do you see what I mean, Sheila?

"Well, yes. But somehow it still bothers me. Doesn't the church have an obligation to teach the moral law?"

Of course it does—because it has an obligation to stand for whatever is true to God's order of creation, and the moral law is part of that truth. But the church has, as her first obligation, the duty to preach the good news—and that, Sheila, is not the law. To sinners, the law is nothing but *bad* news. Only grace can be good. All I'm saying is that our obsession with guilt makes us spend more time on law than on grace; therefore the church has to work harder on grace than on law. Even though she always has to work on both, it's grace that remains her biggest job. But Norman's got his hand up. Norman?

"I'm Norman Keep. I happen to teach English at the university too, but unlike my freewheeling fictional colleague in your parable, Robert, I find myself sympathetic to Sheila's remarks. Let me see if I can point up what I think she's saying.

"I have two children myself. Not as old as Sheila's, but no matter. I think it's the children who are at the root of her objection. Or, better said, the children's moral education. It's not enough just to say that the moral law is one of the eternal truths of God, and that it goes on being true no matter what. Because besides being an eternal truth from God's point of view, it is, for us, a culturally transmitted truth. We're not born with the knowledge of it; we're taught it by the society in which we live. And we're not taught it by a handful of catechetical lectures. Actually the lecture method is probably the least effective approach to moral education. Rather we're taught it by the entire context of word and example in which we find ourselves: parents, peers, parsons, police—whoever.

"It is not enough therefore for me as a parent—or, to the point, Robert, for you as a parson—to maintain that a little theological lip service to an eternally true moral law is sufficient. I teach not only by what I *say* is so, but even more by what I *give the impression* is so. It may be that

[ 155 ]

for persons with fully formed consciences—if indeed there are any such—the preaching of grace will not seem to abrogate the law. But for children?

"I see Sheila nodding her head. I don't know her fifteen-year-old, but the case of any fifteen-year-old seems to fit nicely here. Is such a person's conscience so well formed that it has stopped taking or needing lessons? Take the subject of the morality of sexual acts. I don't want to become mired in any particular development of it—Sheila and I might have some differences here and there. But I think we can all agree that on the basis of any philosophical system, classical, personalist, existentialist, you name it, there will always be some moral lessons that will be judged preferable to others.

"The point is that a teenager, by her very situation in life, is receiving all kinds of instruction, good and bad, in sexual morality—no matter what system you use as a criterion. Does not the parent or the parson in such a case—especially one who claims to know what the true system is—have an obligation, first of all to teach it, and second of all not to allow it to go untaught in the midst of all the competing instruction? Isn't even a seeming indifference to morality—however untrue it may be that it is a real indifference—isn't that almost as bad from a pedagogical standpoint as a principled indifference? Doesn't it just as truly, and perhaps even more subtly, teach a lesson, reinforce a viewpoint, confirm a formation?

"In a word, Robert, my question is, What about moral education: doesn't your radical insistence on grace put the subject in the shade—or even in the dark?"

Ah, Norman. As usual, you go for the jugular. Please note also that he always picks the best spot to spring from. I try to fix your minds on the fire department and I lose you. Norman knows they're on sex and focuses your attention mightily.

All right then: moral education. Let me concede what I think are Norman's valid points.

Yes, the moral law is culturally transmitted. Yes, it is transmitted by impressions as well as by lectures. Yes, the church has an obligation to avoid giving the impression that anything goes. And yes, the preaching of grace without the preaching of law can give just that impression. The New Testament presupposes and fulfills the Old: to present it as divorced from the Old is to present a parody of it. Granted.

That's worth following up, however, because we're in danger of forgetting some distinctions here. We're talking as if grace were addressed to a subject called morality; and that's bound to make mischief. Morality, but its very nature, must be concerned with norms, with standards; whereas grace, by definition, is concerned with persons: it is a refusal to allow the standards to become the basis of their reconciliation or condemnation. Thus the conflict: morality tells you the standard you need to meet in order to be properly alive; grace tells you that all you ultimately need is to be dead—which is either the world's lowest standard or no standard at all.

Grace and morality, therefore, are two different kettles of fish. Morality deals with virtue and vice, with what is strengthening or weakening for human nature considered as an operational possibility. Grace, however, deals with sin, with a condition in which human nature has ceased to be an operational possibility and has ended up a lost cause. Grace is, to say it once again, about raising the dead. In the Bible the opposite of sin is not virtue; it is faith—faith in God who raises the dead.

All this talk about morality, therefore, is misleading. When we get far enough into it we begin to convince ourselves that the preaching of the moral law will, if done energetically enough, lead people to lead good lives and so make them more like what they ought to be. But that's not biblical. St. Paul says that the purpose of the law was not to do that at all, but to bring us to the awareness of our inability to lead good lives, that is, to the awareness of sin. We sit here talking as if proper moral instruction to fifteen-year-olds will somehow keep them clear of sin. But St. Paul says that Scripture has concluded—locked up—*all* under sin, that the promise by faith of Jesus Christ might be given to them that believe.

That's why I called attention to Norman's choice of sexual morality as an illustration: we are so overwound on the subject that it always throws the discussion into confusion. We somehow seriously hope—against all the evidence, mind you—that in the case of sexual behavior our lessons will arm our pupils against lapses. But that just isn't so. We never admit it, of course, but everybody in this room, no matter what his moral education, not only has more of a sex life, mental or otherwise, than the rest of us think, but also has been guilty of breaching whatever sexual ethics he has rather more often than he'd like us to know. That's true in other branches of ethics too: we have all been guilty of breaches of the moral laws against anger, lying, pride and envy. Somehow, though, we manage to be more realistic about them. While we teach our children to tell the truth, for example, we are not terribly surprised when we find them guilty of falsehood; we can even manage to show the little liars some grace without fear of giving the impression that lying is okay. But about sex we're so nervous we derail ourselves.

For openers then, I want you to concede that all the moral instruction in the world, sexual or otherwise, cannot prevent that sin—that death—to which grace is the only answer. Or at least I want you to concede that's what Scripture says. Or if worse comes to worst, I want simply to tell you that is what it says, and that if you think otherwise, you and the Bible have a fight on your hands.

However. Even after you've disabused yourself of the notion that moral education has anything to do with sin prevention, it continues, even on its own terms, to be a problematical subject. The first thing you're tempted to say is that we need it simply because a more moral society is nicer to live in: auto shops don't make unnecessary repairs, butchers keep their thumbs off the scale, plumbers come when they promise, and everyone tells the truth about everything (although when I think of the general level of human performance since Adam, I'm not so sure it would necessarily make for a nicer society to have all that truth flopping around in broad daylight. But let that pass).

If you like, I'll concede the point *materially.* I'll admit that, in fact, if the habit of obeying the law were better inculcated, we'd all be better off. But *formally* I want to wave a cautionary finger. I want you to take a good look at the *principles* by which the law rules over us. Because in fact, there are two of them. The first is the principle of freely chosen obedience to a known good. You love and cherish honesty, for example, and you hate and despise cheating. Those attitudes are in the very fibers of your being; they are part of your substance as a person. Obedience to the law on that principle does indeed produce a more moral society, precisely because it produces truly moral beings: people who have made a free choice of the good. The more types like that you have around, the finer the society they all enjoy.

But not everybody obeys the law on that principle. Society can be divided into three groups: those who freely keep the law, those who freely break the law, and those in the middle somewhere who keep it for fear of what will happen to them if they don't. It strikes me that this third group is probably the largest of the three, and that, in one department or another, everybody here can find himself in it.

What, though, is the principle by which the law rules over that group? Isn't it force? Isn't it intimidation? Isn't it more the response of sheep than human beings? Isn't their *de facto* conformity to the law (which is, admittedly, good for them and for society) more like the enforced order of a police state than the free order of a moral one? Order is order; but not all order is arrived at on a moral basis.

An example. When people complain about the lowering of standards, one of their favorite illustrations is the collapse of marriage as an institution. Society, they say, by tolerating divorce—and the church, by allowing remarriage where she once forbade it—have failed us as moral educators. People were better off in the old days when the church and society had enough clout to make them stay put.

I'll concede part of that: some people who really don't need to jump the matrimonial ship do so nowadays because of difficulties their grandparents would have put up with and turned out the better for. But I deny the rest. The word *clout* was right: a lot of grandmas and grandpas stayed in marriage only because they were afraid of the club the neighbors and the church held over their heads. But that doesn't seem to me much of a triumph of moral education. It has very little of the smell of freely chosen good about it.

There were plenty of people in the good old days who felt nothing but trapped. Some of them, of course, took refuge in the consolations of religion; but watch that line when you're talking morality. The Christian religion is dedicated to the outlandish proposition that Christ cru cified can save you out of any evil whatsoever. It must not be used, however, to advance the idea that the evil he saves you out of somehow turns into a good—that cruci fixion actually becomes a wonderful thing. Keep that up long enough and you can make out a case for burning people's bodies to save their souls. Evil always remains evil in itself, and its natural results are evil too. In fact, therefore, when the inmates of the old matrimonial prison didn't take up religion, they usually made a career of what prisoners are more likely to take up: resentment, bitter ness, self-pity and just plain meanness—none of which look much like the fruits of quality moral education.

But all that's only the first problem with moral educa tion. The second is that it often fails to reach its goal because either the available professors are incompetent or the classroom situation is so full of psychological hangups that the lecturers haven't a chance of being heard. My course to my children on not losing their temper, for ex ample, or yours to your children on not cheating or not dealing in personalities; think about it. Would you serious ly like the faculty evaluation committee of the University of Moral Learning to come around and write a tenure hearing report on the basis of those performances? We'd all be sacked.

But even where we might have some real compe tence—suppose (to unleash Norman's pet dog for a moment) that I am in fact unbelievably good at teaching sexual morality: how far do I get in the subject with these pupils I have brought forth from my own loins, pupils whose sexual identity is scrambled up with mine and for whom seventy years will be too short a time even to begin to sort it all out? If I can't teach my daughter to drive a car without losing the thread of instruction in a tangle of personality conflicts, how am I going to handle a teaching assignment that takes not six half-hour lessons but literally years of daily contact?

But that's enough of that. It is a dismal subject. Worse than economics. Who's next? Mrs. Schlosskaese.

"I'm Gertrude Schlosskaese, and I imagine I'm the oldest person here. What most of you are going through with your children, I'm watching my children go through with theirs. Fortunately, my husband and I can go home after they've had difficult scenes. We sometimes wish there were something we could do to help, but there's really very little room for advice-giving. My oldest son once told me that grandparents have an occupational disease called *gramnesia,* which he defines as the grandparents' tendency to forget that their own children ever did anything as bad as what their grandchildren are doing.

"I just want to say something in favor of what Father has been saying—from the point of view of how I see my own children now. Not so much about grace, but about the freedom I think only grace can give. When I look at my middle-aged children, I feel sad. It seems to me that instead of becoming freer as they've gotten older, they've gotten more and more afraid of failure—to the point where they don't feel they can risk *anything.* And I wonder if that isn't due to the way they were raised—all the emphasis we put on their being acceptable, all the fear of

making mistakes we drummed into them. I see them passing on the same fear. They're wonderful people, successful and very responsible. But they're so depressingly *conventional*, so *tight*, so *tense*. Sometimes I think I must be
turning into a swinger. I was so afraid of their nonconfor-
mity when they were young; now it's their very conformity that frightens me. And the sad part is they don't even
seem to be *happy* in their successes; they seem to be
trapped by them.

"I suppose what I'm saying is that education for freedom is the really important thing—and that the only way
you can give them that is to raise them with the assurance
that they are free to make all the mistakes there are and
still find grace and love every time. That's why I think
Father is right: there *is* something about all this insistence
on law and morality that produces a slave mentality.
Grace really does have to be given more attention. If it
isn't, all we'll see is grown people who are more afraid
than children—and who have to hide from their fear in
work, or drink, or a lot of other things that, as they use
them, are just—well, *joyless.*"

Thank you, Mrs. Schlosskaese. I wouldn't want to
add a word to that. But an illustration just occurred to me
while you were talking about how unhappy, how depress-
ing, how joyless you find the results of not enough grace
in our rearing.

Our trouble is that we always fall into a *legal* framework when we try to understand grace. But that's too
bad, because in a fallen world legality has got to be just
about the most joyless subject there is. So let me try a
completely nonlegal analogy. Let me try an aesthetic one.

Suppose that all of us in this room were magnificently
beautiful people. Not that we haven't plenty of hand-

someness right now, but give us even more: glowing health, trim bodies, gorgeous faces. And give us the manners and the style to match: make our company in this place the most desirable thing imaginable to anybody.

And then postulate a world outside this room that is the exact opposite: ugly people, deformed people, people with their noses eaten off by cancer, people who constantly cough up blood—anything, just so you make it very, very bad. And make them know clearly that, by the measure of our society in here, they are simply unacceptable—that they are, physically, nothing but publicans and sinners who can't come in on any basis whatsoever. But also make them long to come in—to escape the hell of their ugliness and rest here in the heaven of our beauty.

And then give them grace. In spite of their unacceptability, go out into the highways and hedges and compel them to come in. Right now, without waiting for improvements. And with no reservations, no conditions, no holding back. Put away that dreadful coffee pot and break out the champagne and caviar. Retire these ugly steel chairs and bring couches. Get rid of that lo-fi record player and hire Bobby Short.

Now then. Ask yourself a question. Do you seriously think that, in their joy at having been admitted with all their deformity, they will somehow begin to think more kindly of their ugliness? Do you imagine that the man with no nose will suddenly come to the conclusion that he has been given *permission* to have no nose? Do you think he will stop wanting a nose? Can you believe that at this moment of unmerited acceptance he will begin to take pleasure, not in our acceptance of him but in his own noselessness? That he will, as a logical consequence, begin to advocate the cutting off of everybody's nose?

Of course you don't. You know perfectly well that his acceptance in spite of his ugliness will not diminish one bit his desire for a nose. You understand clearly that when Dr. Wonderful, the handsome and omnicompetent plastic surgeon among us, offers to do an infallible nose job on him, he will say yes with all speed, even if it hurts. And he will say yes because he will see no conflict between the law of his beauty and the grace that accepts him in his ugliness, because he will know they are both aimed at the one and only thing we and he are agreed on loving—*at himself.*

But again, enough. I didn't mean to respond to you, Mrs. Schlosskaese; just to thank you and to take off from your note of joy into a happier illustration than the merely legal one. And also, unless I hear violent objections, to bring this coffee hour to a merciful end. I'm sure that by now everyone's thoughts are turning to Sunday drinks and dinner anyway; so allow me, before those more comprehensible goodnesses of God eclipse the subject of theology altogether, one last attempt at summing up.

# 21

It is, I admit, all bizarre. And when it is not bizarre, outrageous—and if not outrageous, then vulgar. Not, mind you, what I have written; rather what I have written about: the gospel of the grace of God that reconciles by raising the dead. Any outlandishness I contributed to the exposition was minor compared to the strangeness of the subject itself; any shock to your sensibilities, a mere nudge compared to the positively rude and bohemian assault launched upon them by God's word of free and unmerited salvation.

For—I hope you see the point at last—the gospel of grace is the end of religion, the final posting of the CLOSED sign on the sweatshop of the human race's perpetual struggle to think well of itself. For that, at bottom, is what religion is: man's well-meant but dim-witted attempt to approve of his unapprovable condition by doing odd jobs he thinks some important Something will thank him for. If he can't offer God a nice Adam, he offers him a nice goat instead—an activity which, as God has pointed out, is an exercise in futility, since it is not possible that the blood of bulls and of goats should take away the entail of a fundamentally worm-eaten self-image.

Religion, therefore, is a loser, a strictly fallen activity. It has a failed past and a bankrupt future. There was no religion in Eden and there won't be any in heaven; and in the meantime Jesus has died and risen to persuade us to knock it all off right now. He has said that as far as God is concerned, we're home free already and there's not a single religious thing you or I have to do about it. We are, as I said a while ago, simply invited to believe that and to cry a little or giggle a lot, as seems appropriate.

In conclusion, therefore, three comments only: one about religion, one about ethics, and one about the life of grace.

*     *     *

I want you to set aside the notion of the Christian religion, because it's a contradiction in terms. You won't learn anything positive about religion from Christianity, and if you look for Christianity in religion, you'll never find it. To be sure, Christianity uses the forms of religion and, to be dismally honest, too many of its adherents act as if it were a religion; but it isn't one, and that's that. The church is not in the religion business; it is in the Gospel-proclaiming business. And the Gospel is the good news that all man's fuss and feathers over his relationship with God is unnecessary because God, in the mystery of the Word who is Jesus, has gone and fixed it up himself. So let that pass.

Think instead of the immemorial religion-type religion of mankind: burning incense at the evening sacrifice, pouring chicken blood on the sacred stone at sunrise. What was that all about? Why did everybody do it? Well, to tell the gospel truth, they did it to fake out a repair job on the hopelessly messed-up inside of their heads, to kid themselves into the impression there was still *something* they could do—in short, to avoid facing the fact that they were dead and only grace could raise them.

And if anyone says, "Ah! but we don't make chicken sacrifices any more," he's lying to himself. We dicker with divinities all day long, whether by bowing down before our self-image or by trying to strike bargains with God himself. The only people who have even a chance of getting out of the sacred stone business are believing Christians—and they spend most of their lives trying to resist the temptation to get back into it. Everybody since Adam is instinctively religious; there's nobody who, left to his own devices, won't burn incense to something.

I told you the story of Paul and Laura to help you see that until the day we can face the fact of our death, we will always try to live by our religion—and that, for as long as we do, our religion will always kill us because, whatever it is, we will sooner or later fail it. Paul's religion of course was romance, not animal sacrifice or the cult of Isis. But it worked the same way. For him, falling in love and being in love was the ultimate, all-justifying act, the perfect sacrifice to his hoked-up image of himself as a man. It redeemed him from the bondage of his otherwise disordered being. If he could be a true acolyte of romance, he did not have to feel so bad about being Paul.

But acolytes must observe the ritual. Their fidelity must be proved by constant attendance at the altar. Suppose, however, they cannot do it? What did Paul do when he found himself unable to boast of his fidelity to the romance with Catharine? Well, he wrote himself off as dead before his god.

On the other hand, acolytes must also worry whether their god is faithful to them. It is not only that their self-esteem requires them to prove themselves to the deity; it is also that the deity must rend the skies and show a smiling face. There must be signs. But if there are not? What happened when Catharine withdrew behind silent heavens? Well, once again, Paul died.

I gave you only five days of Paul's affair with Laura, and only the first five at that. And I promised you no contretemps. But it is no default on that promise to remind you that Paul will not shake his religion of romance quite as easily as he received the fullness of Laura's grace. He will still—perhaps for years, perhaps for life—be tempted to go on seeing his inevitable failure to be a true acolyte of romance as damning evidence of his unacceptability. And all that, even though their relationship came into being solely because of her willingness to bear his unacceptability herself—to undergo, as she put it, a voluntary crucifixion for his sake.

And he will still, for just as long, be tempted to put her to the test, to torment himself and her by demanding signs of divine approval. And when they are not forthcoming—when, for example, either because she just answered the phone out of a deep sleep and made no sense, or because there were children in the room and she couldn't say, "I love you," he does not hear the word his need demands—he will go into an agony of fear at his rejection. And all that, again, in the interest of an idiotic effort to find out if the lover whose grace saved him from the shipwreck of his bookkeeping is herself faithful to the bookkeeping she excused him from.

It is all foolishness. Religion begins after relationship has broken down; the minute anyone reestablishes relationship by grace, it simply ends. It lives only in foul air; when grace cuts off its supply of bus fumes and sewer gas, it coughs itself to death. Paul's joy in love will be in direct proportion to the quickness and thoroughness with which he learns to breathe the fresh air of acceptance; our joy in the love of God will be the same. And our best example will be that other Paul, the Apostle himself, who was the champion bus fume inhaler of all time and still managed to kick the habit. He did successfully with the religion of the law what my Paul was only beginning to do with the religion of romance: he stopped putting himself to the test, and he stopped putting the deity to the test. He finally saw that in a love affair, nobody can earn his way.

Admittedly, he had help. The law he tried to keep was a manifest impossibility; and the God he tried to tempt just wasn't having any: the only sign he got was to be blinded by Jesus until he stopped asking for signs altogether and concentrated on grace. But when he did . . . !

The Epistle to the Romans has sat around the church ever since like a bomb ticking away the death of religion. Every time it's been picked up, the ear-splitting freedom in it has gone off with a roar. The only sad thing is that the church as an institution has spent most of its time playing bomb squad and trying to defuse it. For your comfort, though, it can't be done. Your freedom remains as close to your life as Jesus and as available to your understanding as the nearest copy of St. Paul. Like Augustine therefore, *tolle, lege,* take and read: take the one, read the other, and then hold onto your hat. Compared to that explosion, the clap of doom sounds like a cap pistol.

\*         \*         \*

While we're setting things aside, let's get rid of "Christian" ethics as well as "Christian" religion. Not only because it, too, is a contradiction in terms, but especially because it's a piece of puffery which, given any houseroom at all, elbows the meaning out of both Christianity and ethics.

Ethics is the subdivision of philosophy that deals with moral questions as distinct from, say, logical or ontological ones. As such, it is a strictly human activity. Unlike religion, however, it is not, of itself, a fallen one. It is a natural and proper response of the curious mind of man to the astonishing intricacy of the creation God has set before him. It's a *study,* just as logic is a study; it's an exploration of the wonder of human behavior, just as logic is an exploration of the wonder of human thought. And, like all studies, when it addresses its chosen aspect of reality (in technical language, its *material object*) it does so in the confidence that everybody else who undertakes the same study is likewise addressing the same material object. Whether we investigate ethics or logic, music, gardening, tennis or cookery, we assume that there is something "there" that is the same for all of us—we assume, in short, that dialogue is possible.

To be sure, we all come at that something from different angles—in technical language, again, with different *formal objects* in mind. There is Italian cookery and Chinese cookery, there is French oboe playing and English oboe playing, there is symbolic logic and there is situation ethics. But note two things. First, when oboe players get together, it's oboe playing they're primarily about, not Frenchness or Englishness. Their material object governs the discussion; their formal objects are incidental. But second, there is a limitation as to the range of formal objects that can be admitted. German cookery and Swedish cookery are permissible topics, and so perhaps is even architectural cookery, if you happen to be a whiz at *pastillage* and pulled sugar. But canine cookery? Musical cookery? Symbolic cookery? And what about angelic cookery or divine cookery? Doesn't it look for all the world as if the materiality has been knocked out cold by the application of a totally alien formality? Or else that the formality has been rendered meaningless by its association with inappropriate matter?

That, you see, is the trouble with *Christian* ethics. Of course there will be Christians who study ethics, just as there will be Christians who study cookery, gardening and tennis. And it is entirely possible that their Christianity may lead them to prefer certain ethical, culinary, horticultural or athletic postures to others. It is difficult, however, to see how such preferences could ever lead them to conclude that they had invented something called Christian gardening or Christian tennis. And it is impossible to see how they could imagine there was such a thing as Christian ethics.

Ethics tells you what you ought and ought not to do in order to be recognizably and acceptably human. Christianity tells you about a God who takes unrecognizable and unacceptable human beings and re-cognizes and accepts them in Jesus, whether or not they happen to have done what they ought to have done. Christian ethics is like angelic cookery: nobody in his right mind wants a meal fit for an angel or an angel whose hobby is whipping up omelettes; therefore, nobody in his right mind bothers with the subject at all. Ditto Christian ethics. Christianity and ethics must never be jammed into a single category. All you do by that is destroy both of them. Your Christianity forces you to say that unethical people can go to heaven, and so tempts you to say that ethics is barking up an eschatologically nonexistent tree. And your ethics forces you to say that unethical people are really not what the Creator of the Universe has in mind, thus leading you to question whether a God who so blithely takes them home hasn't, in fact, gone soft in the head.

That, obviously, has been our problem all through this book; and I have deliberately aggravated it so you would see it as a problem and not go on looking at it in your old way as if it were a solution. By hook or by crook or by adulterous parables, I simply had to get you off the bastard subject of Christian ethics. You may—indeed, if you are to be free, you must—take your Christianity neat: grace, straight up, no ice. And you may also—because your sanity and your love of God's creation require it— take your ethics with all the seriousness it deserves: you may strive with might and main to improve your truthfulness, and you will be a better, happier person for it. You may even, by the same token, strive just as hard to perfect your backhand, your French bread or your annual tomato crop—with precisely the same result, because those things are neither more nor less worthy than ethics of your time and attention as a priestly creature in the image of a God who loves them all.

But you may not take the oranges of morality and the apples of the gospel and mush them up into a marmel-sauce called Christian ethics; because if you do, you will lose your grip on the mystery that alone can keep them unique and reconciled. You will, in short, get sick of your weird concoction and go back to imagining you have to choose between them. And the saddest thing about such an unnecessary choice is that, given the way we are, we will usually decide to keep the ethics, which can no more save us than our backhand or our bread, and lose the gospel, which is the only thing that can.

My advice to you therefore is: don't mess with hybrids. Keep a spirited Christian horse and a useful ethical donkey. But don't try to breed a mule. Only a jackass does that.

*        *        *

Let's make a clean sweep of it: let's throw out the idea of "the Christian Life," too. Admittedly, it's not strictly a contradiction in terms like the other two notions, but it's nearly so. The word "Christian" has, through a process of guilt by association, acquired such a freight of religious and ethical meaning that grace, which is the first thing it's about, is almost the last thing people think of when you use it.

I prefer, therefore, to end as I began, with nothing but grace—just as Paul and Laura did, and just as you and I and all the rest do under God. The life of grace is not an effort on our part to achieve a goal we set ourselves. It is a continually renewed attempt simply to believe that someone else has done all the achieving that is needed, and to live in relationship with that person whether we achieve or not. If that doesn't seem like much to you, you're right: it isn't. And as a matter of fact, the life of grace is even less than that. It's not even our life at all, but the life of that someone else rising like the tide in the ruins of our death. For us, it is simply Jesus, Jesus, Jesus, as it was Laura, Laura, Laura for Paul. It is a love affair with an unlosable lover.

And that tells you all you really need to know about it. It tells you that there is only one sin you can commit against it—only one dangerous thing you can ever do—and that is to refuse to believe it. All the rest of its reality is simply a free gift from the other who loves you. Faith—

not "fidelity" but simple trust; not "good faith" but plain belief—is all you need. The gospel of grace is the announcement that all the incomprehensibly good news really is so: you *are* loved, you *are* vindicated, you *are* home. And you are all of that *now,* just because he says so. Trust him.

And when you have done that, you are living the life of grace. No matter what happens to you in the course of that trusting—no matter how many waverings you may have, how many suspicions that you have bought a poke with no pig in it, how much heaviness and sadness your lapses, vices, indispositions and bratty whining may cause you—you believe simply that Somebody Else, by his death and resurrection, has made it all right and you just say thank you and shut up. Your whole slopcloset full of mildewed performances is simply your death; it is Jesus who is your life. If he refused to condemn you because your works were rotten, he certainly isn't going to flunk you because your faith is not so hot. You can fail utterly, therefore, and still live the life of grace. You can fold up physically, spiritually, intellectually or morally and still be safe. Because at the very worst, all you can be is dead— and for him who is the Resurrection and the Life, that just makes you his cup of tea.

That then is the first rule of the life of grace: it is lived out of death. It begins with a solemn proclamation of your death in baptism and it continues all your life long under that same banner: *we believe in the resurrection of the dead.* Death is the operative device that sets us free in Christ—that liberates us from the fear of loss that otherwise dogs our every step. What is it you're afraid of losing? Your wits, your looks, your job, your grip? Your lover, your friends, your standards, your way? Don't be.

Or be, if you feel like it. It doesn't matter. Because you are dead, and your life is hid with Christ in God. The whole package—wits, career, looks, love life, and all the lucky or unlucky stars you may have in your chart—are out of your hands into his. You couldn't keep them if you tried; but in him, you can't lose them except by unfaith. For he says you have them all in him *now*. He says that he is *now* your resurrection and your life—that you are *now* dead and risen in him, that you *now* sit with him in heavenly places—and he asks you simply to trust him about it all. He asks you to believe that in your death you meet him, and that in him nothing is lost. All you do by unfaith is make yourself unavailable to the only Person who ever told you he had it all together.

And that will do for the second rule of the life of grace: your part in it is just to make yourself available. Not to make anything happen. Not to achieve any particular intensity of subjective glow. Certainly not to work yourself up to some objective standard of performance that will finally con God into being gracious. Only to be *there,* and to be open to your lover who, without so much as a by-your-leave, started this whole affair. And your attendance upon him can include literally everything you do because he has accepted it all in the Beloved: all good acts because they are vindicated in him; all rotten acts because they are reconciled in him; and even all religious acts because, in him, they have ceased to be transactions and become celebrations of something already accomplished.

The life of grace is the life of a cripple on an escalator: as far as being able to walk upstairs is concerned, he is simply dead; there is nothing for *him* to do. But then he doesn't need to do anything, because the divine Floor-walker has kindly put him on the eternally moving stair-case of Jesus—and up he goes.

What he does and thinks about himself as he ascends will be delightful or sad or terrifying, depending. Delight-ful, insofar as he celebrates his free ride. Sad, insofar as he fights the escalator. Terrifying, insofar as he forgets he's on it and goes back to dwelling on his own inability to walk. But while all of that will matter to him, none of it will count against him. He's on his way. All he has to do is believe it, and even the sadness and the terror become simply part of the ride up.

And therefore the last rule of the life of grace is that nothing can separate you from it. Not your faults, not your vices, not your being a brat about refusing the cross—not even your rubbing salt in the wounds of Christ or kicking God when he's down. Because he took you by a voluntary crucifixion for your sake, and he takes it all as the price of taking you. Eventually, you will cry over that and those tears will be your repentance. But there isn't even any rush about it. *He knows he loves you,* and that's all that counts. You catch up as you can.

And none of your terrors can separate you from that love either, because they will all, late or soon, go down into your death. You can't hold them forever, and there-fore they won't hold you. In the meantime, of course, they remain terrors, and the death out of which you live by grace remains no fun at all. There will always be more dying than you want and, until your death, there will al-ways be worse jobs of it than you expected. But he says he raises you from them, and if you believe that, you're finally free.

And there, I suppose, is as good an end as any. The only impediment to our freedom is our own unbelief; the only thing that jams out the joy that is set before us is the static of our unwillingness to take the leap into our own death in the faith that Jesus is there. All I can think of to add is that you mustn't even fuss much over your faith either. If only once in your life, for the space of one minute, you trusted him to be there, you would, for that minute, know the joy of your freedom. Even if you never managed to do it again—even if you never managed to do it even that once—it's still true that if he's there, he's there. And if he is, you're free.

In Jesus, we have never been anywhere but on the youngest, freshest day of the new creation. We live in the grace that takes the world between noon and three—at that still point of the turning world where the Word who is our end and our beginning speaks us reconciled in the Land of the Trinity:

> That we too may come to the picnic
> With nothing to hide, join the dance
> As it moves in perichoresis,
> Turns about the abiding tree.

*There is therefore now no condemnation to them that are in Christ Jesus.*